Thomas Carlyle, William Foyé Mozier

The Diamond Necklace

Thomas Carlyle, William Foyé Mozier

The Diamond Necklace

ISBN/EAN: 9783743323506

Manufactured in Europe, USA, Canada, Australia, Japa

Cover: Foto ©ninafisch / pixelio.de

Manufactured and distributed by brebook publishing software (www.brebook.com)

Thomas Carlyle, William Foyé Mozier

The Diamond Necklace

PREFACE.

THE study of Carlyle may be undertaken with profit in the advanced classes of high schools, academies, and preparatory schools. While students are to be warned against the peculiarities and even barbarisms of his style, they may still derive much benefit from the originality, force, and suggestiveness of his thought. After Shakspeare, Carlyle of all English writers furnishes the most abundant material for thought analysis.

The "Diamond Necklace" has been selected for annotation in preference to the more commonly read essays, for several reasons. It presents specimens of all of Carlyle's varied styles: essay, narrative, dramatic, and descriptive. It is, in miniature, a work of the same character as the "French Revolution," Carlyle's most artistic production, and has all the peculiarities, both faulty and beautiful, of that work. It is short and interesting, and experience with it in the class-room has demonstrated the advantages of studying it. Froude, in his life of Carlyle, writes: "The 'Diamond Necklace' . . . in my opinion, is the very finest illustration of Carlyle's literary power." Richard Garnett calls it "a masterpiece of tragi-comedy in narrative, proving that he had all the power needful for the dramatic treatment of history."

Of course the brief biographical sketch introducing this work does not lay claim to completeness or special originality. The student is referred to the best sources of information about Carlyle in the "Bibliography." Numerous notes are necessary to explain Carlyle, because of his figurative style, and the large number of obscure allusions found in his writings.

The introductory "Method of Study" is intended to be suggestive merely. Each teacher, and even each pupil to a certain extent, must be allowed to do his work in his own way.

W. F. MOZIER.

OTTAWA, ILL., Sept. 1, 1892.

CONTENTS.

	PAGE
PREFACE	iii
INTRODUCTION	1
THOMAS CARLYLE	1
EARLY LIFE	1
MRS. CARLYLE AND THE CARLYLES' MARRIED LIFE	6
LIFE AT CRAIGENPUTTOCK, 1828–1834	9
THE DIAMOND NECKLACE	12
LIFE IN LONDON, 1834–1881	13
PORTRAIT AND CHARACTER	17
TEACHINGS AND INFLUENCE	18
LITERARY STYLE	20
BIBLIOGRAPHY	21
CHRONOLOGICAL OUTLINE	23
METHOD OF STUDY	25
THE AFFAIR OF THE DIAMOND NECKLACE	27
SUMMARY OF CONTENTS	31
THE DIAMOND NECKLACE	37
NOTES	141

INTRODUCTION.

THOMAS CARLYLE.

EARLY LIFE.

On the 5th of October, 1795, the "whiff of grapeshot" from the guns of Napoleon silenced the French Revolution. The long agony of anarchy ceased, — to be followed by a military despotism, twenty years of devastating war, the downfall of Napoleon, and a reaction against the principles of the Revolution. Blasted hopes, shattered dreams of an ideal democracy, misery, poverty, exhaustion, discontent, despair, blind gropings after better things, misdirected or hypocritical attempts at reform, characterized the social, political, and spiritual life of Europe in the quarter of a century that followed. In the midst of these times and conditions was born and grew to manhood the historian and essayist who was to describe them in language of fire; the seer and prophet who was to bewail the degeneracy of his age, and draw therefrom the lessons of human life.

Thomas Carlyle was born in the small village of Ecclefechan, Annandale, in the county of Dumfries, Scotland, on the 4th of December, 1795. Although at one time he wished no biography of himself to be written, there is no author whose private or public life is more minutely known. Soon after his death, his executor, James Anthony Froude, published his correspondence and journal, his "Reminiscences," written only for his own private inspection, and the letters and journal of Mrs. Carlyle. Carlyle had not been certain that he wanted any of these published; certainly he did not want them published without revision. He died without having revised them, leaving the question of their publication to the discretion of his executor. This executor, Mr. Froude, published them with practically no revision. Hence we have a picture of Carlyle in all his moods, and the most secret thoughts, feelings, opinions, and incidents of his life are exposed to public gaze. This is very interesting, and undoubtedly gives a complete photograph of the man. Every one, however, has private opinions, states of mind, and freaks of conduct that should be regarded as exempt from publication to the world, and it is unfair to the memory of a great man to make mankind in general as intimately acquainted with him as is his valet, to whom, as the proverb goes, no man is a hero. Perhaps an interesting life of our author could not have been written in any other way, for as far as external occurrences go his life was uneventful. It was devoted to literature entirely. He lived quietly, as a writer of books, first at Craigenputtoch, and then at London, with nothing to disturb him save the general degeneracy of the times — upon which he pours forth the torrents of his wrath — and his neighbors' cats and chickens, which excited his anger no less, perhaps even more.

The birth of the man who was to occupy the high position of "censor of the age" was humble. His father, James Carlyle, was a village mason. "A more remarkable man than my father," says Carlyle, "I have never met in my journey through life; sterling sincerity in thought, word, and deed; most quiet, but capable of blazing into whirlwinds when needful, and such a flash of just insight and brief natural eloquence and emphasis." Both his father and his mother were persons of great force of character and natural strength of mind, though neither was cultured in books. They were simple, upright, self-reliant, deeply religious people. "No man of my day, or hardly any man, can have had better parents," wrote their son. Carlyle's family and family life were always dear to him. He constantly wrote to the different members, especially to his mother, and remembered them with presents and financial aid. Although he had a cynical bearing toward most men, for his father and his mother, his three brothers and his five sisters, he had only the most thoughtful consideration. His deep love for his family is one of the striking elements of his character.

The youthful Thomas learned reading from his mother, and arithmetic from his father. He attended the village school, where he was reported "complete in English" at the age of seven. Latin he learned of the village minister. When he was ten years old, he was sent to the Grammar School at Annan, where he learned French, Latin, a little algebra and geometry, and geography. In "Sartor Resartus," where the history of Teufelsdroeckh is partly autobiographical, Carlyle tells of his hopeful entrance into Annan and of his disagreeable experiences there.

In November, 1809, when he was not yet fourteen, he entered Edinburgh University, expecting in time to enter the ministry. He walked the eighty miles from Ecclefechan to Edinburgh. Here he made some progress in Latin and Greek; he hated philosophy, but studied mathematics with enthusiasm. He did not win any prizes, owing, probably, to a certain diffidence. His most valuable experience at the university was the companionship of a few chosen friends, of whom he was the leader. They all prophesied future greatness for him. Like Macaulay and other men of literature, he devoted more time to general reading in the university library than to the studies of the curriculum. In "Sartor Resartus" he writes:

"I took less to rioting than to thinking and reading, which latter also I was free to do. Nay, from the chaos of that library I succeeded in fishing up more books than had been known to the keeper thereof. The foundation of a literary life was hereby laid. I learned in my own strength to read fluently in almost all cultivated languages, on almost all subjects and sciences. A certain ground-plan of human nature and life began to fashion itself in me, by additional experiments to be corrected and indefinitely extended."

In 1814, having completed the usual course in arts, Carlyle quitted Edinburgh, with the intention of earning his living by teaching until his ordination into the ministry. The next four years of his life were spent in school work, first as mathematical teacher in the burgh school of Annan, afterwards in a somewhat similar position at Kirkaldy. The work of school teaching was distasteful to him. His reserved, impatient, and irritable temperament and his sarcastic speech were not suited to the work. He was neither very popular in the village nor very successful in teaching, though he kept his pupils in awe without the necessity of flogging them. During these years he made the acquaintance of Edward Irving, afterward the noted minister and orator, and of Margaret Gordon, the original of "Blumine" in "Sartor Resartus," with whom he fell in love. His holidays were spent at Mainhill, a farm two miles from Ecclefechan, to which his father had now removed.

In 1818 he resigned his position at Kirkaldy, and having now given up the idea of the ministry, went to Edinburgh to attend law lectures. Then followed what he calls "the three most miserable years" of his life. His studies at Edinburgh, his irregular meals and long fasts had brought on dyspepsia, from which he was now, and continued to be to the end of his life, a constant sufferer. "The cursed hag, dyspepsia," he calls it. "A rat was gnawing at the pit of his stomach."

This made him irritable, nervous, and unhappy, and his exaggerated invectives against the disorder, in his letters home, often needlessly frightened the good people on the farm. In these years, too, he was clouded with doubt and disbelief in the religion of his father. Over these doubts he suffered much anguish of mind, and finally when the crisis came, after "three weeks of total sleeplessness" he found peace. While he was attending the law lectures he tried to make a living by teaching a few pupils and by writing articles for Brewster's "Edinburgh Encyclopædia," sixteen articles in all. He was aided constantly by the sympathy and assistance of his family. During these years he read much in the university library, and diligently studied German, which was to have so important an influence on his thought and his style. His favorite author was Goethe, who seems to have been of great help to his spiritual life. Carlyle had given up the study of law as distasteful, and was again at sea as to his life-work. Yet he seems to have felt that there was something within him of worth, and that ultimately it must find expression in literature. As early as 1814 he had written to a friend: "Yet think not I am careless of literary fame. No; Heaven knows that ever since I have been able to form a wish, the wish of being known has been foremost. O Fortune! thou that givest unto each his portion in this dirty planet, bestow (if it shall please thee) coronets, and crowns, and principalities, and purses, and pudding, and powers upon the great and noble and fat ones of the earth. Grant me that with a heart of independence, unyielding to thy favors and unbending to thy frowns, I may attain to literary fame; and though starvation be my lot, I will smile that I have not been born a king." Those who knew him, even in these obscure days, felt that there was genius there. One of his friends writes, "I hope that the name of Carlyle, at least, will be inseparably connected with the literary history of the nineteenth century." Miss Gordon had written, "Genius will render you great." Irving wrote in 1820, "Would that I could contribute to it [Carlyle's happiness], and one of the richest and most powerful minds I know should not now be struggling with obscurity and a thousand obstacles."

From the gloom and poverty of these Edinburgh experiences, Irving rescued him by securing for him a position as private tutor to the children of the Bullers, a rich Anglo-Indian family. He held this position for two years, giving it up early in 1824. He then visited London and other cities of England, and made a trip to Paris, where he unconsciously gathered impressions for his " French Revolution." During the years 1823-24 he had contributed a " Life of Schiller " to the *London Magazine*, and in 1824 a translation of " Legendre's Geometry," with an original essay on " Proportion." In the same year appeared his translation of Goethe's " Wilhelm Meister," his first notable work. A somewhat unsettled life at Hoddam Hill and at his father's new farm at Scotsbrig was changed now by his marriage to Miss Welsh, of Haddington.

MRS. CARLYLE AND THE CARLYLES' MARRIED LIFE.

Jane Baillie Welsh was born at Haddington, July 14, 1801. Her father, Dr. John Welsh, was a prosperous and cultured gentleman, a descendant of John Knox. Her mother was said to be a descendant of William Wallace. Jane was a bright, witty, lovable, determined little maiden. She learned rapidly at school, and insisted on studying Latin " like a boy." " Jeannie Welsh, the flower of Haddington," she was called. She was in many ways a remarkable woman. She had a fine mind, and had cultivated it to no little extent. A certain wilfulness and capriciousness, together with a habit of brilliant but sharp comment upon unpleasant persons and things, which increased after her association with Carlyle, added piquancy to her character. She had been introduced to Carlyle in 1821 by Irving. Irving had been her teacher, and in time their intimacy grew into a hope that they might marry. This was prevented, however, by Irving's previous engagement to a Miss Martin, from which, though now distasteful to Irving, Miss Martin refused to release him. Carlyle corresponded with Miss Welsh and sent her books. This intimacy soon grew into love on Carlyle's part, and though Miss Welsh thought at first she could not love him sufficiently to marry him, she had great respect and admiration for him, and these finally developed into a feeling that she could marry no one else. They were married at Haddington, Oct. 17, 1826.

The publication of Mrs. Carlyle's letters and journal has exposed all the secret troubles of their married life, and has made it impossible to give a sketch of Carlyle's life and character without considering, in some detail, the character of Mrs. Carlyle, and of the married life of the Carlyles. In these letters Mrs. Carlyle complains bitterly of her lot. After forty years of married life she said, "My dear, whatever you do, never marry a man of genius." She is reported to have said, "I married for ambition, and am miserable." It seems that Carlyle and his wife were, in a sense, unsuited to each other. Undoubtedly each loved the other, yet neither had the ability to call out the expression of that love from the other. Carlyle was absorbed in his work, and paid little attention to his wife, leaving her to do the menial work of the household, the managing of servants, the mending, the cleaning. He had his sphere of literary composition, where, solitary and complaining, he struggled with sublime thoughts; she had her sphere of domestic duties, where, solitary and complaining, she struggled with servants, with cooking, with house vermin. She was undoubtedly fitted for better things. The woman who could write the brilliant letters that she wrote and could daily attract to her drawing-room the wits and wise men of London, must necessarily have felt the drudgery of housework. Yet she had a kind of genius for it, and would have enjoyed it had her husband properly appreciated her efforts. All her sacrifices he seemed to regard as a matter of course, her duty, for the doing of which no thanks were expected. She did and suffered much, that he might live quietly, after his own peculiar manner, and write his books in solitude. She shielded him from the petty annoyances of life. His dyspepsia made him very particular as to the food he ate; she learned to cook that he might have everything to his taste. He was irritable and violent of temper. During their early married life, mealtime brought on a kind of nervous terror for Mrs. Carlyle; for if the meal was cooked properly Carlyle said nothing, but if anything was under-done or over-done, he flew into a rage. He was sensitive to noises; she bribed, wheedled, begged, used every effort to suppress neighboring cocks and other nuisances. While Carlyle looked upon these acts of kindness as a matter of course, it was not because he did not love his wife, but because he was preoccupied with his work, and was naturally undemonstrative. He really had a deep affection for her. "In great matters," she says herself, "he is always kind and considerate; but these little attentions which we women attach so much importance to he was never in the habit of rendering to any one."

If he failed in attention to her and in recognition of her services to him, she too failed as an ideal companion. She did not enter sufficiently into his work. She was nervous, irritable, and sarcastic, as well as he. Indeed, one cause of the unhappiness of their married life was that they were too much alike. Yet after all this has been said, their letters show that they had much pleasure in life. It was only after Mrs. Carlyle's death, when he came to look over her letters and journal, that Carlyle at length realized the unhappiness he had caused her. Then his remorse was heartrending, and his exaggerated imprecations upon himself were pitiable. "Five minutes more of your dear company in this world," he writes in the "Reminiscences." "Oh, that I had you yet but five minutes to tell you all." But he falls back in despair, with the exclamation, "Ah me! Too late, too late." To the world their marriage seemed happy enough, until the published "Reminiscences" and letters after Carlyle's death told all and more than all.

LIFE AT CRAIGENPUTTOCH, 1828–1834.

After their marriage, the Carlyles lived for two years at Comely Bank, Edinburgh, where they made the acquaintance of several literary people, among them Jeffrey, the editor of the *Edinburgh Review*, who accepted Carlyle as a contributor to the *Review*. A few articles on German literature were contributed, but the need of money and the necessity of living cheaply became so pressing that it was decided, much against Mrs. Carlyle's inclinations, to remove to Craigenputtoch, a farm belonging to Mrs. Carlyle.

They went to this place in May, 1828. Craigenputtoch was a lonely moorland farm, situated sixteen miles from Dumfries and a day's journey east of Ecclefechan. "The dreariest spot in all the British isles. The nearest cottage is more than a mile distant from it; the elevation, seven hundred feet above the sea, stunts the trees and limits the garden produce to the hardiest vegetables. The house is gaunt and hungry-looking. It stood with the scanty fields attached as an island in a sea of morass. The landscape is unrelieved either by grace or grandeur, mere undulating hills of grass and heather, with peat bogs in the hollows between them. A sterner spot is hardly to be found in Scotland." (Froude's Life of Carlyle.) For months at a time the Carlyles had no visitors, not even a passing stranger. Mrs. Carlyle said the moors were so still that she could hear the sheep nibbling the grass a quarter of a mile away. Carlyle called it "a devil's den," and a "blasted paradise." In this desolate spot the Carlyles lived for six years, with one servant and an occasional boy to help them. Carlyle wrote in solitude, wrestling with the thoughts that were trying to find expression, often taking long walks and rides on the moor, alone. Mrs. Carlyle's life was far from pleasant. Their lack of money and Carlyle's irritable sensitiveness to household disorder compelled her to cook, scour, mend, and do the work of a servant. She saw too little of her husband, who was absorbed in his work. The work and the loneliness affected her health, and developed, or increased, a nervous disorder from which she was never afterward free. In fact, it finally caused her death. For Carlyle, however, it was a beneficial experience. His health improved, his mind strengthened, his genius developed. He writes in the "Reminiscences:" "We were not unhappy at Craigenputtoch; perhaps these were our happiest days. Useful, continual labor, essentially successful; that makes even the moor green. I found I could do fully twice as much work in a given time there, as with my best effort was possible in London, such the interruptions, etc." He writes to his brother John in 1828: "I write hard all day, and then Jane and I, both learning Spanish for the last month, read a chapter of Don Quixote between dinner and tea, and are already half through the first volume and eager to persevere. After tea I sometimes write again, being dreadfully slow at the business, and then go over to Alick [his brother who was working the farm] and Mary and smoke my last pipe with them; and so I end the day, having done little good perhaps, but almost no ill that I could help to any of

God's creatures. So pass my days, except that sometimes I stroll with my axe or bill in the plantations, and when I am not writing I am reading."

The monotony of their life at Craigenputtoch was varied by a winter spent in London and a second winter in Edinburgh. The Jeffreys came to visit them twice. In 1833 the Carlyles were visited by Emerson, who had turned aside from the beaten paths of travel to talk with a man whose genius he recognized, though it was not yet recognized by Carlyle's countrymen. This visit of Emerson was the beginning of a close friendship, which lasted for nearly fifty years, the correspondence of Emerson and Carlyle being one of the most cheerful features of Carlyle's life. Emerson afterward acted as Carlyle's agent in America, and thus helped him financially at a time when he had great need of such help. Life at Craigenputtoch was enlivened also by letters and presents from Goethe, who appreciated Carlyle's work in German literature and perceived his genius. During the six years at Craigenputtoch, Carlyle contributed to the *Edinburgh Review*, the *Foreign Review*, and *Fraser's Magazine* the articles that now form the first three volumes of his "Miscellanies." At first they were chiefly on German subjects, with the exception of the essay on "Burns," one of Carlyle's best; afterward the subjects were more varied. Carlyle's fortunes had many "ups and downs" during this period. In 1831 we find his popularity on the decline, and Carlyle with only five pounds, and no more expected for months. He had devoted much of his time to the writing of "Sartor Resartus," and this the publishers had refused. It was afterward printed in *Fraser's*. But other articles were received, and fortune revived somewhat. Carlyle was beginning his studies of the French Revolution, with a view to writing on that subject. Ready access to a large library was necessary, and it was finally decided to remove to

London. The last writing of Carlyle's at Craigenputtoch was

THE DIAMOND NECKLACE.

In 1832 Carlyle had contributed an article on "Diderot" to the *Foreign Quarterly*. This had excited interest in the French Revolution, and in 1833, during the winter spent at Edinburgh, he had collected material for articles on "Cagliostro" and the "Diamond Necklace." In March, 1833, he writes his brother: "I am partly minded next to set forth some small narrative about the Diamond Necklace, once so celebrated a business." And later: "I think I shall fasten upon that Necklace business (to prove myself in the narrative style) and commence it (sending for books to Edinburgh) in some few days." He did commence, and two months later, Dec. 24, 1833, he writes: "I have also, with an effort, accomplished the projected piece on the Diamond Necklace. It was finished this day week; really a queer kind of thing, of some forty and odd pages. Jane at first thought we should print it at our own charges, set our name on it, and send it out in God's name. Neither she nor I are now so sure of it, but will consider it. My attempt was to make reality ideal; there is considerable significance in that notion of mine, and I have not yet seen the limit of it, nor shall till I have tried to go as far as it will carry me. The story of the *Diamond Necklace* is all told in that paper with the strictest fidelity, yet in a kind of *musical* way." He offered the article to the *Foreign Quarterly*, but the editor refused it. Carlyle himself calls it "a singular sort of thing, which is very far from pleasing me." He, however, went to work to improve it, reading new books on the subject and making additions; and in February, 1834, we find him writing in his journal, "What to do with that *Diamond Necklace* affair I wrote? must correct it in some points which these new books have illuminated a little." It lay thus awaiting a publisher for three years, but was finally published in *Fraser's Magazine*, in the spring of 1837, a few months before the publication of the " French Revolution." It earned Carlyle little fame and little money, and is not so famous as many of his other works even now, yet it is, in its way, one of the best of his writings.

LIFE IN LONDON, 1834–1881.

The Carlyles arrived in London, and in June, 1834, began housekeeping in the little old-fashioned house at No. 5 Cheyne Row, Chelsea. Carlyle describes it: " We lie safe at a bend of the river, away from all the great roads, have air and quiet hardly inferior to Craigenputtoch, an outlook from the back windows into mere leafy regions with here and there a red high-peaked old roof looking through, and see nothing of London, except by day the summits of St. Paul's Cathedral and Westminster Abbey, and by night the gleam of the great Babylon affronting the peaceful skies. The house itself is probably the best we have ever lived in — a right old, strong, roomy, brick house, built near 150 years ago, and likely to see three races of these modern fashionables fall before it comes down. . . . Chelsea is a singular heterogeneous kind of spot, very dirty and confused in some places, quite beautiful in others, abounding with antiquities and the traces of great men — Sir Thomas More, Steele, Smollett, etc." In this place the Carlyles were to live the remainder of their lives. Here the " Seer of Chelsea " wrote his greatest works, and uttered the oracular warnings that brought pilgrims to No. 5 as to a second Delphi.

The London life of the Carlyles was without stirring experiences. They lived quietly and economically. Old friends and many new ones were constant visitors. Leigh Hunt was their neighbor. John Stuart Mill helped Carlyle in the world of letters. Other friends were John Sterling, whose biography Carlyle wrote, and Lord and Lady Ashburton. Other visitors at the house were Mazzini, Tennyson, Forster, Dickens. Later friends of Carlyle were Ruskin, Froude, Prof. Masson, Prof. Tyndall. Both Carlyle and Mrs. Carlyle frequently made visits with friends outside of London. Indeed, it was Carlyle's practice, after completing a book, to take a long vacation, travelling and visiting his friends. In London, as at Craigenputtoch, Carlyle was absorbed in his work. He left Mrs. Carlyle much to herself, and she felt the loneliness and the household cares. Carlyle was considerably disturbed by neighboring noises, which his wife always succeeded in suppressing. Finally, to be rid of them, he had a sound-proof room constructed at the top of the house, which, alas, proved to be not sound-proof. His dyspepsia and biliousness continued, and the labor of composition was always grievous to him, yet he undoubtedly enjoyed life more than his exaggerated language would lead one to believe.

When Carlyle reached London none of the works that have made him famous had yet been written. Publishers were avoiding him. They recognized a certain genius in him, but had come to the conclusion that it was an erratic genius, which was being wasted upon extravagant nonsense expressed in a barbarous style. In February, 1835, he writes that it is now "some twenty-three months since I have earned one penny by the craft of literature."

All this was changed in 1837 by the publication of the "French Revolution." It was at once recognized as a work of superior merit, and its success was unmistakable. As a vivid, graphic, life-like picture of the Revolution, it has no equal. Its publication marks a new era in history writing.

Carlyle's writings were now no longer rejected by autocratic editors and publishers.

The following year "Sartor Resartus," previously published serially in *Fraser's*, was published in book form. It is a weird, almost grotesque, presentation of Carlyle's philosophy, in which the decayed institutions of society are represented as worn-out clothing, only fit to be cast off.

During these and the following years, Carlyle delivered four courses of public lectures in London on "German Literature," "The History of Literature," "The Revolutions of Modern Europe," and "Hero-Worship." These lectures were received with much delight by fashionable society, Carlyle's broad accent, sing-song delivery, vehement speech, and originality seeming to take hold of the popular taste. In "Chartism" (1839) and "Past and Present" (1843) he attacks the corruptions of modern society and sets forth his opinions of modern reforms. In 1845 appeared the "Life and Letters of Oliver Cromwell," a work that has greatly modified men's opinions of the Protector. Carlyle was now recognized as a leader in literature. His income was ample, his pen feared and respected, his fame assured. "Latter-day Pamphlets" was published in 1850, and the "Life of Sterling" the following year. Carlyle's last great work, taking thirteen years for its completion, was the "History of Frederick II., commonly called the Great," in six volumes, the first two published in 1858, the last in 1865. This work is a marvel of historical research, and its descriptions of battles are so exact and minute that it is said to be used as a text-book by German military students.

Before the completion of this work, Mrs. Carlyle's health had failed alarmingly. Carlyle became aware of her ill health at last, and grew considerate and tender as he had not been before. In 1863 she was knocked down by a cab and injured seriously, but in time was believed to be growing better. In 1865 Carlyle was elected to the rectorship of Edinburgh University, and in April, 1866, went to Edinburgh to deliver the rectorial address. Prof. Tyndall telegraphed to Mrs. Carlyle that the oration was "a perfect triumph." Carlyle lingered in Scotland a few days, and while there received the unexpected and overwhelming news that Mrs. Carlyle had been found dead in her carriage, after taking a drive through the streets of London, the afternoon of April 21.

Carlyle never recovered from this blow, and though he lived fifteen years after the death of his wife, he dwelt secluded and did little work. Mrs. Carlyle was buried at Haddington, where her husband had these words inscribed on her tomb: "Here likewise now rests Jane Welsh Carlyle, Spouse of Thomas Carlyle, Chelsea, London. She was born at Haddington 14th July, 1801, only daughter of the above John Welsh, and of Grace Welsh, Caplegill, Dumfriesshire, his wife. In her bright existence she had more sorrows than are common; but also a soft invincibility, a clearness of discernment, and a loyalty of heart, which are rare. For forty years she was the true and ever-loving helpmate of her husband, and by act and word unweariedly forwarded him, as none else could, in all of worthy, that he did or attempted. She died at London, 21st April, 1865; suddenly snatched away from him, and the light of his life, as if gone out."

His only writings during these fifteen years, were the "Reminiscences," a few articles contributed to magazines, and a series of articles published in one volume, in 1875, on "The Early Kings of Norway," and "The Portraits of John Knox." Palsy of the right hand prevented him from writing several years before his death. He lived, honored at home and abroad, and tenderly cared for by his friends. His powers gradually failed, and he died Feb. 4, 1881. Burial in Westminster Abbey was offered, but this was contrary to his previously expressed wish, and was declined. He was buried at Ecclefechan, in the yard of the old Kirk, where with his beloved parents he sleeps the last sleep.

PORTRAIT AND CHARACTER.

Emerson thus describes Carlyle as he appeared in 1833: "He was tall and gaunt with a cliff-like brow, and holding his extraordinary powers of conversation in easy command; clinging to his northern accent with evident relish; full of lively anecdote, and with a streaming humor which flooded everything he looked upon." A recent biographer, Richard Garnett, describes him as he delivered his lectures in 1837: "There he stood, a spare figure, lacking one inch of six feet; long but compact of head, which seemed smaller than it really was; rugged of feature; brow abrupt like a low cliff, craggy over eyes deep-set, large, piercing, between blue and dark gray, full of rolling fire; firm but flexible lips, no way ungenial; dark, short, thick hair, not crisp, but wavy as rock-rooted, tide-swayed weed; complexion bilious-ruddy or ruddy-bilious, according as Devil or Baker might be prevailing with him."

Carlyle was a man of great force and originality of character. He was sincere above all things. The spirit that dwelt within him was that of truth and hatred of sham. He refused to write popular literature, even though it paid well, because it could not come from him honestly. He chose to write his own convictions in his own way, and brave unpopularity and starvation. His persistency and sincerity at length compelled the world to take him at his own terms. He felt that the times were out of joint, and that it was his mission, as a prophet and teacher, to denounce their falsity and set forth the truth. A motto of his younger days was the emblem of the wasting candle and the inscription, "*Terar, dum prosim*," "Let me be wasted, so I be of use."

He was a strange character. He inherited from his father stern convictions, deep feeling, and a power of metaphorical language. He had a violent temper as a child, and ill health did not improve it. He was irritable, impatient of interruption, and as his mother said, "gey (very) ill to live with." His exaggeration and his metaphorical speech are at times grotesque and humorous. He calls chickens that disturb him "demon fowls;" incompetent servants are "cows," "mooncalves," "scandalous randies." The world is a "dog's cage," a "simmering Tophet," "Pigdom," "Gigmanity." Similar exaggerated and figurative epithets are applied to contemporary authors and to all persons and things that fall within the notice of his cynical, scornful, and sarcastic speech. He was at times deeply depressed and looked with gloom upon the weakness of men and the degeneracy of the times. He could not take a cheerful view of life, and seems to be struggling constantly against its ills, though his habit of exaggeration magnifies the impression of his unhappiness. While his verbal memory was not so wonderful as Macaulay's, his greater originality, his gift of metaphor, his humor, his fluency, made him an equally extraordinary conversationist. Though he always spoke with a broad Annandale accent, his voice was singularly expressive and attractive.

TEACHINGS AND INFLUENCE.

The cardinal doctrines of Carlyle's teachings may be spoken of briefly. "Do thy duty, the duty that lies nearest thee; the next duty will already have become clear." Work, produce, do not lie idle. This teaching of Carlyle's has sometimes been called "the Gospel of Labor." Be true to yourself and to your convictions. Seek the truth. Avoid all sham, hypocrisy, and cant, of which the world, especially the modern world with its false institutions, is so largely composed. Renounce self that you may obey the call of Work and Duty. His political doctrines are not so sound, according to our way of thinking. Democracy he had no faith in. "All things that we see standing accomplished in the world are properly the outer material result, the practical realization and embodiment of Thoughts that dwell in the Great Men sent into the world: the soul of the whole world's history, it may be justly considered, were the history of these." The mass of mankind must bow before these heaven-sent heroes and yield to them implicit obedience. He believed not in the government of the many, but in an aristocracy in the primary sense of that word — a government of the *best*. He had little sympathy with the attempts at reform that he saw made about him, and denounced many of these attempts in violent language. Yet he offers no better way, brings forward no practical method, by which the "vile age of Pinchbeck" may be made less vile.

Carlyle's influence on modern thought has been great. It is the influence, however, of the prophet and exhorter, not of the statesman and the man of action. His work for mankind was to inspire men to act, not to show them how to act. By his powerful and soul-stirring voice he starts men from their lethargy, and bids them be up and doing, though he does not tell them definitely what to do. He comes as one crying in the wilderness, "Prepare ye the way of the Truth." When the Truth has illumined you, what you should do will be made clear. His contribution to humanity and progress lies not in what he has himself accomplished, but in what he has inspired other noble minds to accomplish.

LITERARY STYLE.

The best analysis of Carlyle's style is to be found in Prof. Minto's "Manual of English Prose Literature." A good brief description is the following short extract from Prof. Nichol's "Thomas Carlyle:"—

Carlyle is seldom obscure; the energy of his manner is part of his matter; its abruptness corresponds to the abruptness of his thought, which proceeds often, as it were, by a series of electric shocks that threaten to break through the formal restraints of an ordinary sentence. He writes like one who must, under the spell of his own winged words; at all hazards, determined to convey his meaning; willing like Montaigne, to "despise no phrase of those that run in the streets," to speak in strange tongues, and even to coin new words for the expression of a new emotion. It is his fashion to care as little for rounded phrase as for logical argument, and he rather convinces and persuades by calling up a succession of feelings than by a train of reasoning. . . . He was, let us grant, though a powerful, a one-sided historian, a twisted, though in some aspects a great moralist; but he was in every sense a mighty painter, now dipping his pencil "in the hues of earthquake and eclipse," now etching his scenes with the tender touch of a Millet. . . . The most Protean quality of Carlyle's genius is his humor: now lighting up the crevices of some quaint fancy, now shining over his serious thought like sunshine over the sea, it is at its best as finely quaint as that of Cervantes, more humane than Swift's. There is in it, as in all the highest humor, a sense of apparent contrast, even of contradiction, in life, of matter for laughter in sorrow and tears in joy. He seems to check himself, and, as if afraid of wearing his heart on his sleeve, throws in absurd illustrations of serious propositions, partly to show their universal range, partly in obedience to an instinct of reserve, to escape the reproach of sermonizing and to cut the story short. Carlyle's grotesque is a mode of his golden silence, a sort of Socratic irony in the indulgence of which he laughs at his readers and at himself.

INTRODUCTION. 21

The following analysis is from Leslie Stephens's excellent article on "Carlyle," in the "Dictionary of National Biography:" "His style, whether learned at home or partly acquired under the influence of Irving and Richter (see Froude, i., 396), faithfully reflects his idiosyncrasy. Though his language is always clear, and often pure and exquisite English, its habitual eccentricities offended critics, and make it the most dangerous of models. They are pardonable as the only fitting embodiment of his graphic power, his shrewd insight into human nature, and his peculiar humor, which blends sympathy for the suffering with scorn for fools. His faults of style are the result of the perpetual straining for emphasis of which he was conscious, and which must be attributed to an excessive nervous irritability seeking relief in strong language, as well as to a superabundant intellectual vitality. Conventionality was for him the deadly sin. Every sentence must be alive to its finger's end. As a thinker he judges by intuition instead of calculation. In history he tries to see the essential fact stripped of the glosses of pedants; in politics, to recognize the real forces masked by constitutional mechanism; in philosophy, to hold the living spirit untrammelled by the dead letter."

BIBLIOGRAPHY.

A few of the leading authorities for Carlyle's biography and work are the following: His "Reminiscences," edited by J. A. Froude; Froude's "Life of Carlyle," four volumes; "Letters and Memorials of Jane Welsh Carlyle," edited by Froude; Correspondence of Carlyle and Emerson, edited by Charles Eliot Norton; "Carlyle," in the "Great Writers" series, by Richard Garnett, with an exhaustive bibliography by John P. Anderson, to which the reader is referred; and the article on Carlyle by Leslie Stephens, in the "Dictionary of National Biography," vol. IX. The latest "Life of Carlyle" is by Prof. Nichol, in the "English Men of Letters Series," Harper and Bros., 1892. The innumerable criticisms of Carlyle in the magazines may be found through the guidance of "Poole's Index of Periodical Literature."

CHRONOLOGICAL OUTLINES.

1795. Dec. 4, Carlyle born at Ecclefechan.
1809-14. At Edinburgh University.
1814-16. Mathematical teacher at Annan.
1816-18. Teacher at Kirkaldy.
1818-22. At Edinburgh. Contributes to *Brewster's Edinburgh Encyclopedia*.
1822-24. Tutor to the Bullers.
1824. Translations of *Legendre's Geometry and Trigonometry* and Goethe's *Wilhelm Meister*.
1825. Publishes *Life of Schiller*, previously published in *London Magazine*.
1826. Oct. 17, marries Miss Welsh.
1826-28. At Comely Bank, Edinburgh.
1828-34. At Craigenputtoch. Writes *Sartor Resartus* and *The Diamond Necklace*.
1834. Removes to Chelsea.
1837. *The French Revolution*, his first literary success.
1838. *Sartor Resartus* published.
1839. *Critical and Miscellaneous Essays*.
1840. *Chartism*.
1841. *Heroes and Hero-Worship*.
1843. *Past and Present*.
1845. *Life and Letters of Oliver Cromwell*.
1850. *Latter-day Pamphlets*.
1851. *Life of John Sterling*.
1853. *Occasional Discourse on the Nigger Question*.

1858-65. *History of Frederick the Great.*
1866. Rector's address at Edinburgh.
1866. April 21, death of Mrs. Carlyle.
1867. *Shooting Niagara, and After?*
1874. Receives the Prussian Order of Merit.
1875. *The Early Kings of Norway;* also an *Essay on the Portraits of John Knox.*
1881. Feb. 4, Carlyle dies.

METHOD OF STUDY.

The following method of studying an English classic is suggested to students. Of course there are other methods as good, perhaps better, but it is believed these suggestions will be found helpful. They are made brief intentionally, and cast in the form of rules, that there may be no mistake as to what the student is asked to do.

(*a*.) The first study of the lesson should be a general preliminary reading, without the use of reference books, its object being to get the substance, plot, or "story" of the lesson.

(*b*.) The lesson should then be read a second time, consulting books of reference for the meaning and pronunciation of unfamiliar words, obscure allusions, historical, biographical, and geographical references, etc. Keep a note-book in which are to be recorded the results of these investigations. Make your notes brief, and let them contain only facts essential to the understanding of the text. Do not record many dates. Do not accumulate in your note-books a mass of facts you will not be likely to remember. Transfer to your minds the information contained in your notes. The object of this reading is to gain a complete and intelligent understanding of the meaning of every word and sentence; that is, to grasp the author's thought completely. The books of reference in which most of the information sought for will be found are unabridged dictionaries, especially " Webster's International" and the " Century Dictionary;" Lippincott's " Gazetteer" and "Biographical Dictionary;" Brewer's " Reader's Hand-book" and the same author's "Historic Note-book;" classical and Bible dictionaries; encyclopædias, especially the "Britannica," if its index be consulted.

(c.) Now read the lesson a third time. The new knowledge you will have gained by your second reading will enable you to understand thoroughly what you read and will add a new enjoyment.

(d.) The lesson should now be read critically, for the purpose of analyzing the author's style and qualities as an artist. Note any new characteristics of style that may appear in the lesson and make a record of your observations. Ask yourself such questions as the following: Could the author have expressed his meaning better in such and such a place? Why is such and such an expression particularly appropriate? Wherein, in a notable way, does the author show his art or skill? Has he violated any rules of art? What part does the lesson play in the development of the plot, or the trend of the argument?

(e.) In all your reading use your imagination. As you read, try to call up before your mind a picture of the objects or the scenes described and the incidents narrated. Think while you read. Let your reading be suggestive.

(f.) When reading aloud during the recitation, give special attention to holding the head erect and to reading clearly; remembering that to be a good reader is not to read theatrically, in an unnatural tone, but to read in a straightforward, natural way, with good expression of the sentiment, pronouncing correctly and enunciating clearly.

(g.) Passages that please you or "familiar quotations" should be memorized, for the purpose of training the memory and of enriching the mind.

(h.) Special work in outlining, abstracting, characterization, biography of the author, composition, etc., should be frequently assigned by the instructor.

THE AFFAIR OF THE DIAMOND NECKLACE.

AMONG the host of miserable mistakes and crimes that preceded the French Revolution, exciting hostile public opinion and intense hatred of the monarchy and existing institutions, the affair of the Diamond Necklace is prominent.

Prince Louis de Rohan was a profligate, wealthy, and vain cardinal of the church. He had been Ambassador of France at Vienna under Louis XV., and while there had incurred the displeasure of the Empress Maria Theresa and of her daughter, Marie Antoinette, then recently married to the Dauphin of France. When Marie Antoinette became queen at the accession of Louis XVI., Rohan was recalled from Vienna and banished from the court at Versailles. To a man of his character of mind and way of living this was little short of perpetual imprisonment. He made every effort to regain the favor of the queen and to restore himself at court, but in vain.

About this time one Boehmer, court jeweller of France, had made a beautiful necklace composed of five hundred diamonds and valued at one million eight hundred thousand livres, or between four hundred and four hundred and fifty thousand dollars. He tried to sell this magnificent diamond necklace to the king, but the queen refused it on the ground of expense. Poor Boehmer was distracted, and his vehement efforts to sell the necklace became a court joke. At this stage of affairs an adventuress came to his assistance.

Jeanne de Saint-Remi was an illegitimate descendant of the royal house of Valois. She had married a *gendarme* named Lamotte, and by virtue of her descent now called him Count, and herself Countess de Lamotte. Living by hook or crook and buzzing about the outer circles of the court, she learned of the troubles of both Rohan and Boehmer, and a colossal and daring project of fraud shaped itself in her brain. Gaining the acquaintance of Rohan in January, 1784, she duped him into believing that she was intimate with the queen and that the queen wanted the diamond necklace. Cagliostro, a noted astrologer and magician, was called in to befuddle further the brain of the vain and foolish cardinal.

Rohan was led to believe that the queen wished him to act as her agent in purchasing the necklace, which the king would not allow her to purchase; that she would afterward pay for it in instalments; and that for his assistance in the matter he would be restored to her favor, and ultimately admitted to court. All was to be secret for the present, however. A rascal named Villette was admitted to the fraudulent game, and his part was to forge notes from the queen to Rohan, and to act the part of the queen's valet. The cardinal was completely deceived. He believed that he was fully in the favor of the queen. To confirm him in this belief the countess contrived a fictitious interview between Rohan and the queen, in the Hornbeam Arbor of the garden at Versailles. A Parisian street girl, Gay D'Oliva, who somewhat resembled Marie Antoinette in figure and profile, impersonated the queen — the darkness and a skilfully contrived interruption preventing the cardinal from discovering the deception.

The result of all this was, that on the 29th of January, 1785, Boehmer and Rohan signed an agreement by which the latter was to purchase the necklace for the queen, and pay for it in five equal instalments, the first in six months. On Feb. 1, the necklace was delivered to Rohan, and the next evening, in Lamotte's apartments at Versailles, in the presence of the cardinal, it was delivered to Villette, supposed by Rohan to be the queen's valet. The necklace now vanished forever. Lamotte, the husband, and Villette went abroad and sold the diamonds in London and in Amsterdam.

Meantime the cardinal was growing anxious at not receiving recognition for his services from the queen. The day of the first payment, July 30, came, and no instalment from the queen. Boehmer, importunate for his money, spoke to the king's minister, and the whole daring and successful plot was exposed. The cardinal was arrested Aug. 15, Assumption Day, as he was about to celebrate mass, and was imprisoned in the Bastille. Lamotte and Villette had escaped, but the "Countess" de Lamotte, Gay D'Oliva, Cagliostro and his wife, were arrested and imprisoned. The trial lasted nine months and ended May 31, 1786. The cardinal was acquitted and completely exonerated. Madame Lamotte was found guilty, was branded with a V (*voleuse*, thief), and was to be confined in the Salpetrière. Lamotte, though out of reach of the sentence, was condemned to the galleys for life. Villette was banished from France. The rest were acquitted.

The trial caused immense scandal. The powerful families of Rohan, Soubise, and Condé, and the people of France, generally, sided with the cardinal and blamed the queen, falsely charging her with being a party to the plot. The miserable business still further undermined respect for the throne and increased the unpopularity of Marie Antoinette. The odium of the "Diamond Necklace" imbittered all her future life, and followed her to the very steps of the guillotine.

Of the authorities on the Necklace matter quoted by Carlyle, the best and most easily accessible is an edition of the "Memoirs of Marie Antoinette, by Madame Campan," edited by Lamartine, with appendices containing copious extracts from the "Memoirs" of Georgel. Accounts of the intrigue are given, in Tytler's "Marie Antoinette;" in the Encyclopedia Britannica, article "Rohan;" in Chambers's Encyclopedia, article "Diamond Necklace;" in Guizot's "History of France." Carlyle's "French Revolution" will throw light on parts of the "Diamond Necklace."

SUMMARY OF CONTENTS.

THE DIAMOND NECKLACE.

CHAP. I. *The Age of Romance.*

THE Age of Romance can never cease: All Life romantic, and even miraculous.—How few men have the smallest turn for *thinking!* "Dignity" and deadness of History: Stifling influence of Respectability. No age ever seemed romantic to itself. Perennial Romance: The lordliest Real-Phantasmagoria, which men name *Being*. What fiction can be so wonderful, as the thing that *is?* The Romance of the *Diamond Necklace* no foolish brainweb, but actually "spirit-woven" in the Loom of Time.

CHAP. II. *The Necklace is made.*

Last infirmity of M. Boehmer's mind: The King's Jeweller would fain be maker of the Queen of Jewels. Difference between *making* and agglomerating: The various Histories of those several Diamonds: What few things *are* made by man. A Necklace, fit only for the Sultana of the World.

CHAP. III. *The Necklace cannot be sold.*

Miscalculating Boehmer! The Necklace intended for the neck of Du Barry; but her foul day is now over. Many praises, but no purchaser. Loveliest Marie-Antoinette, every inch a Queen. The Age of Chivalry gone, and that of Bankruptcy is come.

Chap. IV. *Affinities: the Two Fixed-ideas.*

A man's little Work lies not isolated, stranded; but is caught-up by the boundless Whirl of Things, and carried — who shall say whither? Prince Louis de Rohan; a nameless Mass of delirious Incoherences, held-in a little by conventional Politesse. These are thy gods, O France! Sleek Abbé Georgel, a model Jesuit, and Prince de Rohan's nursing-mother. Embassy to Vienna: Disfavor of Maria Theresa and of the fair Antoinette. — Hideous death of King Louis the Well-beloved. Rohan returns from Vienna; and the young Queen refuses to see him. Teetotum-terrors of life at Court. His Eminence's blank despair, and desperate struggle to clutch the favor he has lost. Give the wisest of us a "fixed-idea," and what can his wisdom help him! — Will not her Majesty buy poor Boehmer's Necklace? and oh, will she not smile once more on poor dissolute, distracted Rohan? The beautiful clear-hearted Queen, alas, beset by two Monomaniacs; whose "fixed-ideas" may one day meet.

Chap. V. *The Artist.*

Jeanne de Saint-Remi, a brisk little nondescript Scion-of-Royalty: Her parentage and hungry prospects. Her singularly undecipherable character. Conscience not essential to every character named human. A Spark of vehement Life, not developed into Will of any kind, only into Desires of many kinds: Glibness, shiftiness and untamability. — Kittenness not yet hardened into cathood. Marries M. de Lamotte, and dubs him Count. Hard shifts for a living. Visits his Eminence Prince Louis de Rohan; his monomaniac folly now under Cagliostro's management. The glance of hungry genius.

Chap. VI. *Will the Two Fixed-ideas meet?*

The poor Countess de Lamotte's watergruel rations; and desperate tackings and manœuvrings within wind of Court. Eminence Rohan arrives thitherward, driven by his fixed-idea. Idle gossiping and tattling concerning Boehmer and his Necklace. In some moment of inspiration, a question rises on our brave Lamotte: If not a great Divine Idea, then a great Diabolic one. How Thought rules the world!—A female Dramatist worth thinking of. Could Madame de Lamotte have written a *Hamlet?* Poor Eminence Rohan in a Prospero's-grotto of Cagliostro magic; led on by our sprightly Countess's soft-warbling deceitful blandishments.

Chap. VII. *Marie-Antoinette.*

The Countess plays upon the credulity of his Eminence: Strange messages for and from the innocent, unconscious Queen. Frankhearted Marie-Antoinette; beautiful Highborn, so foully hurled low! The "Sanctuary of Sorrow" for all the wretched: That wild-yelling World, and all its madness, will one day lie dumb behind thee!

Chap. VIII. *The Two Fixed-ideas will unite.*

Further dexterities of the glib-tongued Lamotte: How she managed with Cagliostro. Boehmer is made to hear (by accident) of her new found favor with the Queen; and believes it. Drowning men catch at straws, and hungry blacklegs stick at nothing. — *Can* her Majesty be persuaded to buy the Necklace? *Will* her Majesty deign to accept a present so worthy of her? — Walk warily, Countess de Lamotte, with nerve of iron, but on shoes of felt!

CHAP. IX. *Park of Versailles.*

Ineffable expectancy stirs-up his Eminence's soul: "This night the Queen herself will meet thee!" Sleep rules this Hemisphere of the World; — rather curious to consider. Darkness and magical delusions: The Countess's successful dramaturgy. Ixion de Rohan, and the foul Centaurs he begat.

CHAP. X. *Behind the Scenes.*

The Lamotte all-conquering talent for intrigue. The Demoiselle d'Oliva; unfortunate Queen's Similitude, and unconscious tool of skilful knavery.

CHAP. XI. *The Necklace is sold.*

A pause: The two fixed-ideas have felt each other, and are rapidly coalescing. His Eminence will buy the Necklace, on her Majesty's account. O Dame de Lamotte! — "I? Who saw me in it?" — Rohan and Boehmer in earnest business conference: A forged Royal approval: Secrecy as of Death.

CHAP. XII. *The Necklace vanishes.*

The bargain concluded; his Eminence the proud possessor of the Diamond Necklace. Again the scene changes; and he has forwarded it — whither he little dreams.

CHAP. XIII. *Scene Third: by Dame de Lamotte.*

Cagliostro, with his greasy prophetic bulldog face. Countess de Lamotte and his Eminence in the Versailles Gallery.

Through that long Gallery, what figures have passed, and vanished! The Queen now passes; and graciously looks this way, according to her habit: Dame de Lamotte looks on, and dexterously pilfers the royal glances. Eminence de Rohan's helpless, bottomless, beatific folly.

CHAP. XIV. *The Necklace cannot be paid.*

The Countess's Dramaturgic labors terminate. How strangely in life the Play goes on, even when the Mover has left it! No Act of man can ever die. His Eminence finds himself no nearer his expected goal: Unspeakable perturbations of soul and body. — Blacklegs in full feather: Rascaldom has no strong-box. Dame de Lamotte gayly stands the brunt of the threatening Earthquake: The farthest in the world from a brave woman. — Gloomy weather-symptoms for his Eminence: A thunder-clap (*per* Countess de Lamotte); and mud-explosion beyond parallel.

CHAP. XV. *Scene Fourth: by Destiny.*

Assumption-day at Versailles; — a thing they call worshipping God to enact: All Noble France, waiting only the signal to begin worshipping. Eminence de Rohan chief-actor in the imposing scene. Arrestment in the King's name: There will be no Assumption-service this day. The Bastille opens its iron bosom to all the actors in the Diamond-drama.

CHAP. XVI. *Missa est.*

The extraordinary "Necklace Trial," an astonishment and scandal to the whole world. Prophetic Discourse by Count Arch-Quack Cagliostro: — Universal Empire of Scoundrelism:

Truth wedded to Sham gives birth to Respectability. The old Christian whim, of some sacred covenant with an actual, living and ruling God. Scoundrel Worship and Philosophy: Deep significance of the Gallows. Hideous fate of Dame de Lamotte. Unfortunate foully-slandered Queen: Her eyes red with their first tears of pure bitterness. The Empire of Imposture in flames. — This strange, many-tinted Business, like a little cloud from which wise men boded Earthquakes.

THE DIAMOND NECKLACE.[1]

[1837.]

CHAPTER I.

AGE OF ROMANCE.

THE Age of Romance has not ceased; it never ceases; it does not, if we will think of it, so much as very sensibly decline. "The passions are repressed by social forms; great passions no longer show themselves?" Why, there are passions still great enough to replenish Bedlam, for it never wants tenants; to suspend men from bed-posts, from improved-drops at the west end of Newgate. A passion that explosively shivers asunder the Life it took rise in, ought to be regarded as considerable: more no passion, in the highest heyday of Romance, yet did. The passions, by grace of the Supernal and also of the Infernal Powers (for both have a hand in it), can never fail us.

And then, as to "social forms," be it granted that they are of the most buckram quality, and bind men up into

[1] FRASER'S MAGAZINE, Nos. 85 and 86.

the pitifullest, straitlaced, commonplace existence, — you ask, Where is the Romance? In the Scotch way one answers, Where is it not? That very spectacle of an Immortal Nature, with faculties and destiny extending through Eternity, hampered and bandaged up, by nurses, pedagogues, posture-masters, and the tongues of innumerable old women (named "force of public opinion"); by prejudice, custom, want of knowledge, want of money, want of strength, into, say, the meagre Pattern-Figure that, in these days, meets you in all thoroughfares: a "god-created Man," all but abnegating the character of Man; forced to exist, automatized, mummy-wise (scarcely in rare moments audible or visible from amid his wrappages and cerements), as Gentleman or Gigman; and so selling his birthright of Eternity for the three daily meals, poor at best, which Time yields: — is not this spectacle itself highly romantic, tragical, if we had eyes to look at it? The high-born (highest-born, for he came out of Heaven) lies drowning in the despicablest puddles; the priceless gift of Life, which he can have but *once*, for he waited a whole Eternity to be born, and now has a whole Eternity waiting to see what he will do when born, — *this* priceless gift we see strangled slowly out of him by innumerable packthreads; and there remains of the glorious Possibility, which we fondly named Man, nothing but an inanimate mass of foul loss and disappointment, which we wrap in shrouds and bury underground, — surely with well-merited tears. To the Thinker here lies Tragedy enough; the epitome and marrow of all Tragedy whatsoever.

But so few are Thinkers? Ay, Reader, so few think; there is the rub! Not one in the thousand has the smallest turn for thinking; only for passive dreaming and hearsaying, and active babbling by rote. Of the eyes that men do glare withal so few can *see*. Thus is the world become such a fearful confused Treadmill; and each man's task has got entangled in his neighbor's, and pulls it awry; and the Spirit of Blindness, Falsehood and Distraction, justly named the Devil, continually maintains himself among us; and even hopes (were it not for the Opposition, which by God's grace will also maintain itself) to become supreme. Thus too, among other things, has the Romance of Life gone wholly out of sight: and all History, degenerating into empty invoice-lists of Pitched Battles and Changes of Ministry; or still worse, into "Constitutional History," or "Philosophy of History," or "Philosophy teaching by Experience," is become dead, as the Almanacs of other years, — to which species of composition, indeed, it bears, in several points of view, no inconsiderable affinity.

"Of all blinds that shut-up men's vision," says one, "the worst is Self." How true! How doubly true, if Self, assuming her cunningest, yet miserablest disguise, come on us, in never-ceasing, all-obscuring reflexes from the innumerable Selves of others; not as Pride, not even as real Hunger, but only as Vanity, and the shadow of an imaginary Hunger for Applause; under the name of what we call "Respectability!" Alas now for our Historian: to his other spiritual deadness (which however, so long as he physically breathes, cannot be considered *complete*) this sad new magic influence is added! Henceforth his Histories must all be screwed up into the "dignity of History." Instead of looking fixedly at the *Thing*, and first of all, and beyond all, endeavoring to *see* it, and fashion a living Picture of it, not a wretched politico-metaphysical Abstraction of it, he has now quite other matters to look to. The Thing lies shrouded, invisible, in thousandfold hallucinations, and foreign air-images: What did the Whigs say of it? What did the Tories? The Priests? The Freethinkers? Above all, What will my own listening circle say of *me* for what I say of it? And then his Respectability in general, as a literary gentleman; his not despicable talent for philosophy! Thus is our poor Historian's faculty directed mainly on two objects: the Writing and the Writer, both of which are quite extraneous; and the Thing written-of fares as we see. Can it be wonderful that Histories, wherein open lying is not permitted, are unromantic? Nay, our very Biographies, how stiff starched, foisonless, hollow! They stand there respectable; and — what more? Dumb idols; with a skin of delusively painted wax-work; inwardly empty, or full of rags and bran. In our England especially, which in these days is become the chosen land of Respectability, Life-writing has dwindled to the sorrowfullest condition; it requires a man to be some disrespectable, ridiculous Boswell before he can write a tolerable Life. Thus too, strangely enough, the only Lives worth reading are those of Players, emptiest and poorest of the sons of

Adam; who nevertheless were sons of his, and brothers of ours; and by the nature of the case, had already bidden Respectability good-day. Such bounties, in this as in infinitely deeper matters, does Respectability shower down on us. Sad are thy doings. O *Gig;* sadder than those of Juggernaut's Car: that, with huge wheel, suddenly crushes asunder the bodies of men; thou in thy light-bobbing Long-Acre springs, gradually winnowest away their souls!

Depend upon it, for one thing, good Reader. no age ever seemed the Age of Romance to *itself.* Charlemagne, let the Poets talk as they will, had his own provocations in the world: what with selling of his poultry and pot-herbs, what with wanton daughters carrying secretaries through the snow; and, for instance, that hanging of the Saxons over the Weserbridge (four thousand of them they say, at one bout), it seems to me that the Great Charles had his temper ruffled at times. Roland of Roncesvalles too, we see well in thinking of it, found rainy weather as well as sunny; knew what it was to have hose need darning; got tough beef to chew, or even went dinnerless; was saddle-sick, calumniated, constipated (as his madness too clearly indicates); and oftenest felt, I doubt not, that this was a very Devil's world, and he, Roland himself, one of the sorriest caitiffs there. Only in long subsequent days, when the tough beef, the constipation and the calumny had clean vanished, did it all begin to seem Romantic, and your Turpins and Ariostos found music in it. So, I say, is it *ever!* And the more, as your true hero, your true Roland, is ever *unconscious* that he is a hero: this is a condition of all greatness.

In our own poor Nineteenth Century, the Writer of these lines has been fortunate enough to see not a few glimpses of Romance; he imagines his Nineteenth is hardly a whit less romantic than that Ninth, or any other since centuries began. Apart from Napoleon, and the Dantons, and the Mirabeaus, whose fire-words of public speaking, and fire-whirlwinds of cannon and musketry, which for a season darkened the air, are perhaps at bottom but superficial phenomena, he has witnessed, in remotest places, much that could be called romantic, even miraculous. He has witnessed overhead the infinite Deep, with greater and lesser lights, bright-rolling, silent-beaming, hurled forth by the Hand of God: around him and under his feet, the wonderfullest Earth, with her winter snow-storms and her summer spice-airs; and, unaccountablest of all, *himself* standing there. He stood in the lapse of Time; he saw Eternity behind him, and before him. The all-encircling mysterious tide of FORCE, thousandfold (for from force of Thought to force of Gravitation what an interval!) billowed shoreless on; bore him too along with it,—he too was part of it. From its bosom rose and vanished, in perpetual change, the lordliest Real-Phantasmagory, which men name *Being;* and ever anew rose and vanished; and ever that lordliest many-colored scene was full, another yet the same. Oak-trees fell, young acorns sprang: Men too, new-sent from the Unknown, he met, of tiniest size, who waxed into stature, into strength of sinew, passionate fire and light: in other men the light was growing dim, the sinews all feeble; then sank, motionless, into ashes, into invisibility; returned *back* to the Unknown, beckoning him their mute farewell. He wanders still by the parting-spot; cannot hear *them;* they are far, how far! — It was a sight for angels, and archangels; for, indeed, God himself had made it wholly. One many-glancing asbestos-thread in the Web of Universal-History, spirit-woven, it rustled there, as with the howl of mighty winds, through that "wild-roaring Loom of Time." Generation after generation, hundreds of them or thousands of them from the unknown Beginning, so loud, so stormful-busy, rushed torrent-wise, thundering down, down; and fell all silent, — nothing but some feeble re-echo, which grew ever feebler, struggling up; and Oblivion swallowed them *all*. Thousands more, to the unknown Ending, will follow: and *thou* here, of this present one, hangest as a drop, still sungilt, on the giddy edge; one moment, while the Darkness has not yet ingulfed thee. O Brother! is *that* what thou callest prosaic; of small interest? Of small interest and for *thee?* Awake poor troubled sleeper: shake off thy torpid nightmare-dream; look, see, behold it, the Flame-image; splendors high as Heaven, terrors deep as Hell: this is God's Creation; this is Man's Life! — Such things has the Writer of these lines witnessed, in this poor Nineteenth Century of ours; and what are all such to the things he yet hopes to witness? Hopes, with truest assurance. "I have painted so much," said the good Jean Paul, in his old days, "and I have never seen the Ocean; the Ocean of Eternity I shall not fail to see!"

Such being the intrinsic quality of this Time, and of all Time whatsoever, might not the Poet who chanced to walk through it find objects enough to paint? What object soever he fixed on, were it the meanest of the mean, let him but paint it in its actual truth, as it swims there, in such environment; world-old, yet new and never-ending; an indestructible portion of the miraculous All, — his picture of it were a Poem. How much more if the object fixed on were not mean, but one already wonderful; the mystic "actual truth" of which, if it lay not on the surface, yet shone through the surface, and invited even Prosaists to search for it!

The present Writer, who unhappily belongs to that class, has nevertheless a firmer and firmer persuasion of two things: first, as was seen, that Romance exists; secondly, that now, and formerly, and evermore it exists, strictly speaking, in Reality alone. The thing that *is*, what can be *so* wonderful; what, especially to us that *are*, can have such significance? Study Reality, he is ever and anon saying to himself; search out deeper and deeper *its* quite endless mystery: see it, know it; then, whether thou wouldst learn from it, and again teach; or weep over it, or laugh over it, or love it, or despise it, or in any way relate thyself to it, thou hast the firmest enduring basis: *that* hieroglyphic page is one thou canst read on forever, find new meaning in forever.

Finally, and in a word, do not the critics teach us: "In whatsoever thing thou hast thyself felt interest, in

that or in nothing hope to inspire others with interest"?
— In partial obedience to all which, and to many other principles, shall the following small Romance of the *Diamond Necklace* begin to come together. A small Romance, let the reader again and again assure himself, which is no brainweb of mine, or of any other foolish man's; but a fraction of that mystic "spirit-woven web," from the "Loom of Time," spoken of above. It is an actual Transaction that happened in this Earth of ours. Wherewith our whole business, as already urged, is to paint it truly.

For the rest, an earnest inspection, faithful endeavor has not been wanting, on our part; nor, singular as it may seem, the strictest regard to chronology, geography (or rather in this case, topography), documentary evidence, and what else true historical research would yield. Were there but on the reader's part a kindred openness, a kindred spirit of endeavor! Beshone strongly, on both sides, by such united two-fold Philosophy, this poor opaque Intrigue of the *Diamond Necklace* might become quite translucent between us; transfigured, lifted up into the serene of Universal-History; and might hang there like a smallest Diamond Constellation, visible without telescope, — so long as it could.

CHAPTER II.

THE NECKLACE IS MADE.

HERR, or as he is now called Monsieur, Boehmer, to all appearance wanted not that last infirmity of noble and ignoble minds — a love of fame; he was destined also to be famous more than enough. His outlooks into the world were rather of a smiling character: he has long since exchanged his guttural speech, as far as possible, for a nasal one; his rustic Saxon fatherland for a polished city of Paris, and thriven there. United in partnership with worthy Monsieur Bassange, a sound practical man, skilled in the valuation of all precious stones, in the management of workmen, in the judgment of their work, he already sees himself among the highest of his guild: nay, rather the very highest, — for he has secured, by purchase and hard money paid, the title of King's Jeweller; and can enter the Court itself, leaving all other Jewellers, and even innumerable Gentlemen, Gigmen and small Nobility, to languish in the vestibule. With the costliest ornaments in his pocket, or borne after him by assiduous shopboys, the happy Boehmer sees high drawing rooms and sacred *ruelles* fly open, as with talismanic *Sesame;* and the brightest eyes of the whole world grow brighter: to him alone of men the Unapproachable reveals herself in mysterious *négligée;* taking and giving counsel. Do not, on all gala-days and gala-nights, his works praise him? On the gorgeous robes of State, on Court-dresses and Lords' stars, on the diadem of Royalty: better still, on the swan-neck of Beauty, and her queenly garniture from plume-bearing aigrette to shoe-buckle on fairy-slipper, — that blinding play of colors is Boehmer's doing: he is *Joaillier-Bijoutier de la Reine.*

Could the man but have been content with it! He could not: Icarus-like, he must mount too high; have his wax-wings melted, and descend prostrate, — amid a cloud of vain goose-quills. One day, a fatal day (of some year, probably among the *Seventies* of last Century), it struck Boehmer: Why should not I, who as Most Christian King's Jeweller, am properly first Jeweller of the Universe, — make a Jewel which the Universe has not matched? Nothing can prevent thee, Boehmer, if thou have the skill to do it. Skill or no skill, answers he, I have the ambition: my Jewel, if not the beautifulest, shall be the dearest. Thus was the Diamond Necklace determined on.

Did worthy Bassange give a willing, or a reluctant consent? In any case he consents; and co-operates. Plans are sketched, consultations held, stucco models made; by money or credit the costliest diamonds come in; cunning craftsmen cut them, set them: proud Boehmer sees the work go prosperously on. Proud man! Behold him on a morning after breakfast: he has stepped down to the innermost workshop, before sallying out; stands there with his laced three-cornered hat, cane under arm; drawing-on his gloves: with nod, with nasal-guttural word, he gives judicious confirmation, judicious abnegation, censure and approval. A still joy is dawning over that bland, blond face of his; he can think, while in many a sacred boudoir he visits the Unapproachable, that an *opus magnum,* of which the world wotteth not, is progressing. At length comes a morning when care has terminated, and joy can not only dawn but shine; the Necklace, which shall be famous and world-famous, is made.

Made we call it, in conformity with common speech, but properly it was not made; only, with more or less spirit of method, arranged and agglomerated. What spirit of method lay in it, might be made; nothing more. But to tell the various Histories of those various Diamonds, from the first making of them; or even, omitting all the rest, from the first digging of them in the far Indian mines! How they lay, for uncounted ages and æons (under the uproar and splashing of such Deucalion Deluges, and Hutton Explosions, with steam enough, and Werner Submersions), silently imbedded in the rock; did nevertheless, when their hour came, emerge from it, and first beheld the glorious Sun smile on them, and with their many-colored glances smile back on him. How they served next, let us say, as eyes of Heathen Idols, and received worship. How they had then, by fortune of war or theft, been knocked out; and exchanged among camp-sutlers for a little spirituous liquor, and bought by Jews, and worn as signets on the fingers of tawny or white Majesties; and again been lost, with the fingers too, and perhaps life (as by Charles the Rash, among the mud-ditches of Nancy), in old-forgotten glorious victories: and so, through innumerable varieties of fortune, — had come at last to the cutting-wheel of Boehmer: to be united, in strange fellowship, with comrades also blown together from all ends of the Earth, each with a history of its own! Could these aged stones, the youngest of them Six Thousand years of age and upwards, but have spoken, *there* were an Experience for Philosophy to teach by!— But now, as was said, by little caps of gold, and daintiest rings of the same, they are all being, so to speak, enlisted under Boehmer's flag, — made to take rank and file, in new order, no Jewel asking his neighbor whence he came; and parade there for a season. For a season only; and then — to disperse, and enlist anew *ad infinitum*. In such inexplicable wise are Jewels, and Men also, and indeed all earthly things, jumbled together and asunder, and shovelled and wafted to and fro, in our inexplicable chaos of a World. This was what Boehmer called *making* his Necklace.

So, in fact, do other men speak, and with even less reason. How many men, for example, hast thou heard talk of making money; of making, say, a million and a half of money: Of which million and a half, how much if one were to look into it, had they *made?* The accurate value of their Industry; not a sixpence more. Their making, then, was but, like Boehmer's, a clutching and heaping together;— by-and-by to be followed also by a dispersion. Made? Thou too vain individual! were these towered ashlar edifices; were these fair bounteous leas, with their bosky umbrages and yellow harvests; and the sunshine that lights them from above, and the granite rocks and fire-reservoirs that support them from below, made by *thee?* I think, by another. The very shilling that thou hast was dug, by man's force, in Carinthia and Paraguay; smelted sufficiently; and stamped, as would seem, not without the advice of our late Defender of the Faith, his Majesty George the Fourth. Thou hast it, and holdest it; but whether, or in what sense, thou hast *made* any farthing of it, thyself canst not say. If the courteous reader ask, What things, then, are made by man? I will answer him, Very few indeed. A Heroism, a Wisdom (a god-given Volition that has realized itself), is made now and then: for example, some five or six Books, since the Creation, have been made. Strange that there are not more: for surely every encouragement is held out. Could I, or thou, happy reader, but make one, the world would let us keep it unstolen for Fourteen whole years, — and take what we could get for it.

But, in a word, Monsieur Boehmer has made his Necklace, what he calls made it: happy man is he. From a Drawing, as large as reality, kindly furnished by "Taunay, Printseller, of the Rue d'Enfer;" and again, in late years, by the Abbé Georgel, in the Second Volume of his *Mémoires* curious readers can still fancy to themselves what a princely Ornament it was. A row of seventeen glorious diamonds, as large almost as filberts, encircle, not too tightly, the neck, a first time. Looser, gracefully fastened thrice to these, a three-wreathed festoon, and pendants enough (simple pear-shaped, multiple star-shaped, or clustering amorphous) encircle it, enwreath it, a second time. Loosest of all, softly flowing round from behind in priceless catenary, rush down two broad threefold rows; seem to knot themselves, round a very Queen of Diamonds, on the bosom; then rush on, again separated, as if there were length in plenty; the very tassels of them were a fortune for some men. And now lastly, two other inexpressible threefold rows, also with their tassels, will, when the Necklace is on and clasped, unite themselves behind into a doubly inexpressible *six*fold row; and so stream down, together or asunder, over the hind-neck, — we may fancy, like lambent Zodiacal or Aurora-Borealis fire.

All these on a neck of snow slight-tinged with rose-bloom, and within it royal Life: amidst the blaze of lustres; in sylphish movements, espièglerics, coquetteries, and minuet-mazes; with every movement a flash of star-rainbow colors, bright almost as the movements of the fair young soul it emblems! A glorious ornament; fit only for the Sultana of the World. Indeed, only attainable by such; for it is valued at 1,800,000 livres; say in round numbers, and sterling money, between eighty and ninety thousand pounds.

CHAPTER III.

THE NECKLACE CANNOT BE SOLD.

MISCALCULATING Boehmer! The Sultana of the Earth shall never wear that Necklace of thine; no neck, either royal or vassal, shall ever be the lovelier for it. In the present distressed state of our finances, with the American War raging round us, where thinkest thou are eighty thousand pounds to be raised for such a thing? In this hungry world, thou fool, these five hundred and odd Diamonds, good only for looking at, are intrinsically worth less to us than a string of as many dry Irish potatoes, on which a famishing Sansculotte might fill his belly. Little knowest thou, laughing Joaillier-Bijoutier, great in thy pride of place, in thy pride of *savoir-faire*, what the world has in store for thee. Thou laughest there; by-and-by thou wilt laugh on the wrong side of thy face mainly.

While the Necklace lay in stucco effigy, and the stones of it were still "circulating in Commerce," Du Barry's was the neck it was meant for. Unhappily, as all dogs male and female, have but their day, her day is done; and now (so busy has Death been) she sits retired, on mere half pay, without prospects, at Saint-Cyr. A generous France will buy no more neck-ornaments for *her:*—O Heaven! the Guillotine-axe is already forging (North, in Swedish Dalecarlia, by sledge-hammers and fire; South too, by taxes and *tailles*) that will shear her neck in twain!

But, indeed, what of Du Barry? A foul worm; hatched by royal heat, on foul composts, into a flaunting butterfly; now diswinged, and again a worm! Are there not Kings' Daughters and Kings' Consorts; is not Decoration the first wish of a female heart,—often also, if such heart is empty, the last? The Portuguese Ambassador is here, and his rigorous Pombal is no longer Minister: there is an Infanta in Portugal, purposing by Heaven's blessing to wed.—Singular! the Portuguese Ambassador, though without fear of Pombal, praises, but will not purchase.

Or why not our own loveliest Marie-Antoinette, once Dauphiness only; now every inch a Queen: what neck in the whole Earth would it beseem better? It is fit only for her.—Alas, Boehmer! King Louis has an eye for diamonds; but he too is without overplus of money: his high Queen herself answers queenlike, "We have more need of Seventy-fours than of Necklaces." *Laudatur et alget!*—Not without a qualmish feeling, we apply next to the Queen and King of the Two Sicilies. In vain, O Boehmer! In crowned heads there is no hope for thee. Not a crowned head of them can spare the eighty thousand pounds. The age of Chivalry is gone, and that of Bankruptcy is come. A dull, deep, presaging movement rocks all thrones: Bankruptcy is beating down the gate, and no Chancellor can longer barricade her out. She will enter; and the shoreless fire-lava of DEMOCRACY is at her back! Well may Kings, a second time, "sit still with awful eye," and think of far other things than Necklaces.

Thus for poor Boehmer are the mournfullest days and nights appointed; and this high-promising year (1780, as we laboriously guess and gather) stands blacker than all others in his calendar. In vain shall he, on his sleepless pillow, more and more desperately revolve the problem; it is a problem of the insoluble sort, a true "irreducible case of Cardan:" the Diamond Necklace will not sell.

CHAPTER IV.

AFFINITES: THE TWO FIXED-IDEAS.

Nevertheless, a man's little Work lies not isolated, stranded; a whole busy World, a whole native-element of mysterious never-resting Force, environs it; will catch it up; will carry it forward, or else backward: always, infallibly, either as living growth, or at worst as well-rotted manure, the Thing Done will come to use. Often, accordingly, for a man that had finished any little work, this were the most interesting question: In such a boundless whirl of a world, what hook will it be, and what hooks, that shall catch up this little work of mine; and whirl *it* also, — through such a dance? A question, we need not say, which, in the simplest of cases, would bring the whole Royal Society to a nonplus. — Good Corsican Letitia! while thou nursest thy little Napoleon, and he answers thy mother-smile with those deep eyes of his, a world-famous French Revolution, with Federations of the *Champ de Mars*, and September Massacres, and Bakers' Customers *en queue*, is getting ready: many a Danton and Desmoulins; prim-visaged, Tartuffe-looking Robespierre, as yet all schoolboys; and Marat weeping bitter rheum, as he pounds horsedrugs, — are preparing the fittest arena for him!

Thus too, while poor Boehmer is busy with those Diamonds of his, picking them "out of Commerce," and his craftsmen are grinding and setting them; a certain ecclesiastical Coadjutor and Grand Almoner, and prospective Commendator and Cardinal, is in Austria, hunting and giving suppers; for whom mainly it is that Boehmer and his craftsmen so employ themselves. Strange enough, once more! The foolish Jeweller at Paris, making foolish trinkets; the foolish Ambassador at Vienna, making blunders and debaucheries: these Two, all uncommunicating, wide asunder as the Poles, are hourly forging for each other the wonderfullest hook-and-eye; which will hook them together, one day, — into artificial Siamese-Twins, for the astonishment of mankind.

Prince Louis de Rohan is one of those select mortals born to honors, as the sparks fly upwards; and, alas, also (as all men are) to troubles no less. Of his genesis and descent much might be said, by the curious in such matters; yet perhaps, if we weigh it well, intrinsically little. He can, by diligence and faith, be traced back some handbreadth or two, some century or two; but after that, merges in the mere "blood-royal of Brittany;" long, long on this side of the Northern Immigrations, he is not so much as to be sought for; — and leaves the whole space onwards from that, into the bosom of Eternity, a blank, marked only by one point, the Fall of Man! However, and what alone concerns us, his kindred, in these quite recent times, have been much about the Most Christian Majesty; could there pick up what was going. In particular, they have had a turn of some continuance for Cardinalship and Commendatorship. Safest trades these, of the calm, do-nothing sort: in the do-something line, in Generalship, or such like (witness poor Cousin Soubise, at Rosbach), they might not fare so well. In any case, the actual Prince Louis, Coadjutor at Strasburg, while his uncle the Cardinal-Archbishop has not yet deceased, and left him his dignities, but only fallen sick, already takes his place on one grandest occasion: he, thrice-happy Coadjutor, receives the fair, young, trembling Dauphiness, Marie-Antoinette, on her first entrance into France; and can there, as Ceremonial Fugleman, with fit bearing and semblance (being a tall man, of six-and-thirty), do the needful. Of his other performances up to this date, a refined History had rather say nothing.

In fact, if the tolerating mind will meditate it with any sympathy, what could poor Rohan perform? Performing needs light, needs strength, and a firm clear footing; all of which had been denied him. Nourished, from birth, with the choicest physical spoon-meat, indeed; yet also, with no better spiritual Doctrine and Evangel of Life than a French Court of Louis the Well-beloved could yield; gifted moreover, and this too was but a new perplexity for him, with shrewdness enough to see through much, with vigor enough to despise much; unhappily, not with vigor enough to spurn it from him, and be forever enfranchised of it, — he awakes, at man's stature, with man's wild desires, in a World of the merest incoherent Lies and Delirium; himself a nameless Mass of delirious Incoherences,—covered over at most, and held in a little, by conventional Politesse, and a Cloak of prospective Cardinal's Plush. Are not intrigues, might Rohan say, the industry of this our Universe; nay, is not the Universe itself, at bottom, properly an intrigue? A Most Christian Majesty, in the *Parc-aux-cerfs*; he, thou seest, is the god of this lower world; in the fight of Life, our war-banner and celestial *En-touto-nika* is a Strumpet's Petticoat: these are thy gods, O France! — What, in such singular circumstances, could poor Rohan's creed and world-theory be, that he should "perform" thereby? Atheism? Alas, no; not even Atheism: only Machiavellism; and the indestructible faith that "ginger is hot in the mouth." Get ever new and better *ginger*, therefore; chew it ever the more diligently: 'tis all thou hast to look to, and that only for a day.

Ginger enough, poor Louis de Rohan: too much of ginger! Whatsoever of it, for the five senses, money, or money's worth, or backstairs diplomacy, can buy; nay for the sixth sense too, the far spicier ginger, Antecedence of thy fellow-creatures, — merited, at least, by infinitely finer housing than theirs. Coadjutor of Strasburg, Archbishop of Strasburg, Grand Almoner of France, Commander of the Order of the Holy Ghost, Cardinal Commendator of St. Wast d'Arras (one of the fattest benefices here below): all these shall be housings for Monseigneur: to all these shall his Jesuit Nursing-mother, our vulpine Abbé Georgel, through fair court-weather and through foul, triumphantly bear him; and

wrap him with them, fat, somnolent Nursling as he is.
— By the way, a most assiduous, ever-wakeful Abbé is
this Georgel; and wholly Monseigneur's. He has scouts
dim-flying, far out, in the great deep of the world's business; has spider-threads that overnet the whole world;
himself sits in the centre, ready to run. In vain shall
King and Queen combine against Monseigneur: "I was
at M. de Maurepas' pillow before six," — persuasively
wagging my sleek coif, and the sleek reynard-head under
it; I managed it all for him. Here too, on occasion of
Reynard Georgel, we could not but reflect what a singular species of creature your Jesuit must have been.
Outwardly, you would say, a man; the smooth semblance
of a man: inwardly, to the centre, filled with stone!
Yet in all breathing things, even in stone Jesuits, are
inscrutable sympathies: how else does a Reynard Abbé
so loyally give himself, soul and body, to a somnolent
Monseigneur; — how else does the poor Tit, to the
neglect of its own eggs and interests, nurse up a huge
lumbering Cuckoo; and think its pains all paid, if the
sootbrown Stupidity will merely grow bigger and bigger!
— Enough, by Jesuitic or other means, Prince Louis de
Rohan shall be passively kneaded and baked into Commendator of St. Wast and much else; and truly *such* a
Commendator as hardly, since King Thierri, first of the
Fainéans, founded that Establishment, has played his
part there.

Such, however, have Nature and Art combined together to make Prince Louis. A figure thrice-clothed
with honors; with plush, and civic and ecclesiastic gar-

niture of all kinds; but in itself little other than an amorphous congeries of contradictions, somnolence and violence, foul passions and foul habits. It is by his plush cloaks and wrappages mainly, as above hinted, that such a figure sticks together: what we call "coheres," in any measure; were it not for these, he would flow out boundlessly on all sides. Conceive him farther, with a kind of radical vigor and fire, for he can see clearly at times, and speak fiercely; yet left in this way to stagnate and ferment, and lie overlaid with such floods of fat material: have we not a true image of the shamefullest Mud-volcano, gurgling and sluttishly simmering, amid continual steamy indistinctness, — except as was hinted, in wind-*gusts;* with occasional terrifico-absurd mud-explosions!

This, garnish it and fringe it never so handsomely, is, alas, the intrinsic character of Prince Louis. A shameful spectacle: such, however, as the world has beheld many times; as it were to be wished, but is not yet to be hoped, the world might behold no more. Nay, are not all possible delirious incoherences, outward and inward, summed up, for poor Rohan, in this one incrediblest incoherence, that *he*, Prince Louis de Rohan, is named Priest, Cardinal of the Church? A debauched, merely libidinous mortal, lying there quite helpless, *di*ssolute (as we well say); whom to see Church *Cardinal*, symbolical *Hinge* or main Corner of the Invisible Holy in this World, an Inhabitant of Saturn might split with laughing, — if he did not rather swoon with pity and horror!

THE DIAMOND NECKLACE. 61

Prince Louis, as ceremonial fugleman at Strasburg, might have hoped to make some way with the fair young Dauphiness; but seems not to have made any. Perhaps, in those great days, so trying for a fifteen-years Bride and Dauphiness, the fair Antoinette was too preoccupied: perhaps, in the very face and looks of Prospective-Cardinal Prince Louis, her fair young soul read, all unconsciously, an incoherent *Roué*-ism, bottomless Mud-volcanoism; from which she by instinct rather recoiled.

However, as above hinted, he is now gone, in these years, on Embassy to Vienna: with "four-and-twenty pages" (if our remembrance of Abbé Georgel serve) "of noble birth," all in scarlet breeches; and such a retinue and parade as drowns even his fat revenue in perennial debt. Above all things, his Jesuit Familiar is with him. For so everywhere they must manage: Eminence Rohan is the cloak, Jesuit Georgel the man or automaton within it. Rohan, indeed, sees Poland a-partitioning; or rather Georgel, with his "masked Austrian" traitor "on the ramparts," sees it for him: but what can he do? He exhibits his four-and-twenty scarlet pages, — who, we find, "smuggle" to quite unconscionable lengths; rides through a Catholic procession, Prospective-Cardinal though he be, because it is too long and keeps him from an appointment; hunts, gallants; gives suppers, Sardanapalus-wise, the finest ever seen in Vienna. Abbé Georgel, as we fancy it was, writes a Despatch in his name "every fortnight;" — mentions in one of these, that "Maria Theresa stands, indeed, with the handkerchief in one hand, weeping for the woes of Poland; but with the sword in the other hand, ready to cut Poland in sections, and take her share." Untimely joke; which proved to Prince Louis the root of unspeakable chagrins! For Minister D'Aiguillon (much against his duty) communicates the Letter to King Louis; Louis to Du Barry, to season her *souper*, and laughs over it: the thing becomes a court joke; the filially-pious Dauphiness hears it, and remembers it. Accounts go, moreover, that Rohan spake censuringly of the Dauphiness to her Mother: this probably is but hearsay and false; the devout Maria Theresa disliked him, and even despised him, and vigorously labored for his recall.

Thus, in rosy sleep and somnambulism, or awake only to quaff the full wine cup of the Scarlet Woman his Mother, and again sleep and somnambulate, does the Prospective-Cardinal and Commendator pass his days. Unhappy man! This is not a world which was made in sleep; which it is safe to sleep and somnambulate in. In that "loud-roaring Loom of Time" (where above nine hundred millions of hungry Men, for one item, restlessly weave and work), so many threads fly humming from their "eternal spindles;" and swift invisible shuttles, far darting, to the Ends of the World, — complex enough! At this hour, a miserable Boehmer in Paris, whom thou wottest not of, is spinning, of diamonds and gold, a paltry thrum that will go nigh to strangle the life out of thee.

Meanwhile Louis the Well-beloved has left, forever, his *Parc-aux-cerfs;* and, amid the scarce-suppressed hootings of the world, taken up his last lodging at St. Denis. Feeling that it was all over (for the small-pox has the victory, and even Du Barry is off), he, as the Abbé Georgel records, " made the *amende honorable* to God " (these are his Reverence's own words) ; had a true repentance of three days' standing ; and so, continues the Abbé, " fell asleep in the Lord." Asleep in the Lord, Monsieur l'Abbé ! If such a mass of Laziness and Lust fell asleep in the Lord, *who*, fanciest thou, is it that falls asleep — elsewhere ? Enough that he did fall asleep ; that thick-wrapt in the Blanket of the Night, under what keeping we ask not, *he* never through endless Time can, for his own or our sins, insult the face of the Sun any more ; — and so now we go onward, if not to less degrees of beastliness, yet at least and worst, to cheering varieties of it.

Louis XVI. therefore reigns (and, under the Sieur Gamain, makes locks) ; his fair Dauphiness has become a Queen. Eminence Rohan is home from Vienna ; to condole and congratulate. He bears a letter from Maria Theresa ; hopes the Queen will not forget old Ceremonial Fuglemen, and friends of the Dauphiness. Heaven and Earth ! The Dauphiness Queen will not see him ; orders the Letter to be *sent* her. The King himself signifies briefly that he " will be asked for when wanted ! "

Alas ! at Court, our motion is the delicatest, unsurest. We go spinning, as it were, on teetotums, by the edges of bottomless deeps. Rest is fall ; so is one false whirl. A moment ago, Eminence Rohan seemed waltzing with the best : but, behold, his teetotum has *carried him over;*

there is an inversion of the centre of gravity; and so now, heels uppermost, velocity increasing as the time, space as the square of the time, — he rushes.

On a man of poor Rohan's somnolence and violence, the sympathizing mind can estimate what the effect was. Consternation, stupefaction, the total jumble of blood, brains and nervous spirits; in ear and heart, only universal hubbub and louder and louder singing of the agitated air. A fall comparable to that of Satan! Men have, indeed, been driven from Court; and borne it, according to ability. Choiseul, in these very years, retired Parthianlike, with a smile or scowl; and drew half the Court-host along with him. Our Wolsey, though once an *Ego et Rex meus*, could journey, it is said, without strait-waistcoat, to his monastery; and there telling beads, look forward to a still longer journey. The melodious, too soft-strung Racine, when his King turned his back on him, emitted one meek wail, and submissively — died. But the case of Coadjutor de Rohan differed from all these. No loyalty was in him, that he should die; no self-help, that he should live; no faith, that he should tell beads. His is a mud-volcanic character; incoherent, mad, from the very foundation of it. Think too, that his Courtiership (for how could any nobleness enter there?) was properly a gambling speculation: the loss of his trump Queen of Hearts can bring nothing but flat unredeemed despair. No other game has he, in this world, — or in the next. And then the exasperating *Why?* The *How came it?* For that Rohanic, or Georgelic, sprightliness of the "handkerchief in one hand, and sword in the other," if indeed that could have caused it all, has quite escaped him. In the name of Friar Bacon's Head, *what* was it? Imagination, with Desperation to drive her, may fly to all points of Space;—and returns with wearied wings, and no tidings. Behold *me here:* this, which is the first grand certainty for man in general, is the first and last and only one for poor Rohan. And then his *Here!* Alas, looking upwards, he can eye, from his burning marl, the azure realms, once his; and Cousin Countess de Marsan, and so many Richelieus, Polignacs, and other happy angels, male and female, all blissfully gyrating there; while he—!

Nevertheless hope, in the human breast, though not in the diabolic, springs eternal. The outcast Rohan bends all his thoughts, faculties, prayers, purposes, to one object; one object he will attain, or go to Bedlam. How many ways he tries; what days and nights of conjecture, consultation; what written unpublished reams of correspondence, protestation, backstairs diplomacy of every rubric! How many suppers has he eaten; how many given,—in vain! It is his morning song, and his evening prayer. From innumerable falls he rises; only to fall again. Behold him even, with his red stockings, at dusk, in the Garden of Trianon: he has bribed the Concierge; will see her Majesty in spite of Etiquette and Fate; peradventure, pitying his long sad King's-evil, she will touch him and heal him. In vain,— says the Female Historian, Campan. The Chariot of Majesty shoots rapidly by, with high-plumed heads in it; Eminence is known by his red stockings, but not looked at, only laughed at, and left standing like a Pillar of Salt.

Thus through ten long years, of new resolve and new despondency, of flying from Saverne to Paris, and from Paris to Saverne, has it lasted; hope deferred making the heart sick. Reynard Georgel and Cousin de Marsan, by eloquence, by influence, and being "at M. de Maurepas' pillow before six," have secured the Archbishropric, the Grand Almonership; the Cardinalship (by the medium of Poland); and, lastly, to tinker many rents, and appease the Jews, that fattest Commendatorship, founded by King Thierri the Do-nothing — perhaps with a view to such cases. All good! languidly croaks Rohan; yet all not the one thing needful; alas, the Queen's eyes do not yet shine on me.

Abbé Georgel admits, in his own polite diplomatic way, that the Mud-volcano was much agitated by these trials; and in time quite changed. Monseigneur deviated into cabalistic courses, after elixirs, philtres, and the philosopher's stone; that is, the volcanic steam grew thicker and heavier: at last by Cagliostro's magic (for Cagliostro and the Cardinal by elective affinity must meet), it sank into the opacity of perfect London fog! So too, if Monseigneur grew choleric, wrapped himself up in reserve, spoke roughly to his domestics and dependents, — were not the terrifico-absurd mud-explosions becoming more frequent? Alas, what wonder? Some nine-and-forty winters have now fled over his Eminence (for it is 1783), and his beard falls white to the shaver; but age for him brings no "benefit of experience." He is possessed by a fixed-idea!

Foolish Eminence! is the Earth grown all barren and of a snuff color, because one pair of eyes in it look on thee askance? Surely thou hast thy Body there yet: and what of soul might from the first reside in it. Nay, a warm, snug Body, with not only five senses (sound still, in spite of much tear and wear), but most eminent clothing, besides; — clothed with authority over much, with red Cardinal's cloak, red Cardinal's hat; with Commendatorship, Grand-Almonership, so kind have thy Fripiers been; with dignities and dominions too tedious to name. The stars rise nightly, with tidings (for thee too, if thou wilt listen) from the infinite Blue; Sun and Moon bring vicissitudes of season; dressing green, with flower-borderings, and cloth of gold, this ancient ever-young Earth of ours, and filling her breasts with all-nourishing mother's milk. Wilt thou work? The whole Encyclopædia (not Diderot's only, but the Almighty's) is there for thee to spread thy broad faculty upon. Or, if thou have no faculty, no Sense, hast thou not, as already suggested, Senses, to the number of five? What victuals thou wishest, command; with what wine savoreth thee, be filled. Already thou art a false lascivious Priest; with revenues of, say, a quarter of a million sterling; and no mind to mend. Eat, foolish Eminence; eat with voracity, — leaving the shot till *afterwards!* In all this the eyes of Marie Antoinette can neither help thee nor hinder.

And yet what is the Cardinal, dissolute mud-volcano

though he be, more foolish herein, than all Sons of
Adam? Give the wisest of us once a "fixed-idea," —
which, though a temporary madness, who has not had?
— and see where his wisdom is! The Chamois-hunter
serves his doomed seven years in the Quicksilver Mines;
returns salivated to the marrow of the backbone; and
next morning — goes forth to hunt again. Behold Cardalion King of Urinals; with a woful ballad to his mistress' eyebrow! He blows out, Werter-wise, his foolish
existence, because *she* will not have it to keep; — heeds
not that there are some five hundred millions of other
mistresses in this noble Planet; most likely much such
as she. O foolish men! They sell their Inheritance
(as their Mother did hers), though it is Paradise, for
a crotchet: will they not, in every age, dare not only
grapeshot and gallows-ropes, but Hell-fire itself, for better sauce to their victuals? My friends, beware of fixed-ideas.

Here, accordingly, is poor Boehmer with one in his
head too! He has been hawking his "irreducible case
of Cardan," that Necklace of his, these three long years,
through all Palaces and Ambassadors' Hotels, over the
old "nine Kingdoms," or more of them than there now
are: searching, sifting Earth, Sea and Air, for a customer. To take his Necklace in pieces; and so, losing
only his manual labor and expected glory, dissolve his
fixed-idea, and fixed diamonds, into current ones: this
were simply casting out the Devil — from himself; a
miracle, and perhaps more! For he too has a Devil, or
Devils: one mad object that he strives at; that he too

will attain, or go to Bedlam. Creditors, snarling, hound him on from without; mocked Hopes, lost Labors, bearbait him from within: to these torments his fixed-idea keeps him chained. In six-and-thirty weary revolutions of the Moon, was it wonderful the man's brain had got dried a little?

Behold, one day, being Court-Jeweller, he too bursts, almost as Rohan had done, into the Queen's retirement, or apartment; flings himself (as Campan again has recorded) at her Majesty's feet; and there, with clasped uplifted hands, in passionate nasal-gutturals, with streaming tears and loud sobs, entreats her to do one of two things: Either to buy his Necklace; or else graciously to vouchsafe him her royal permission to drown himself in the River Seine. Her Majesty, pitying the distracted bewildered state of the man, calmly points out the plain third course: *Dépécez votre Collier*, Take your Necklace in pieces; — adding withal, in a tone of queenly rebuke, that if he would drown himself, he at all times could, without her furtherance.

Ah, *had* he drowned himself, with the Necklace in his pocket; and Cardinal Commendator at his skirts! Kings, above all, beautiful Queens, as far-radiant Symbols on the pinnacles of the world, are so exposed to madmen. Should these two fixed-ideas that beset this beautifullest Queen, and almost burst through her Palace-walls, one day *unite*, and this *not* to jump into the River Seine: — what maddest result may be looked for!

CHAPTER V.

THE ARTIST.

If the reader has hitherto, in our too figurative language, seen only the figurative hook and the figurative eye, which Boehmer and Rohan, far apart, were respectively fashioning for each other, he shall now see the cunning Milliner (an actual, unmetaphorical *Milliner*) by whom these two individuals, with their two implements, are brought in contact, and hooked together into stupendous artificial Siamese-Twins; — after which the whole nodus and solution will naturally combine and unfold itself.

Jeanne de Saint-Remi, by courtesy or otherwise, Countess styled also *of Valois*, and even *of France*, has now, in this year of Grace 1783, known the world for some seven-and-twenty summers; and had crooks in her lot. She boasts herself descended, by what is called *natural* generation, from the Blood-Royal of France: Henri Second, before that fatal tourney-lance entered his right eye and ended him, appears to have had, successively or simultaneously, four — unmentionable women: and so, *in vice* of the third of these, came a certain Henri de Saint-Remi into this world; and, as High and Puissant Lord, ate his victuals and spent his days, on an allotted domain of Fontette, near Bar-sur-Aube, in Champagne. Of High and Puissant Lords, at this Fontette, six other generations followed; and thus ultimately, in a space of some two centuries,— succeeded in realizing this brisk little Jeanne de Saint-Remi, here in question. But, ah, what a falling-off! The Royal Family of France has well nigh forgotten its left-hand collaterals: the last High and Puissant Lord (much clipt by his predecessors), falling into drink, and left by a scandalous world to drink his pitcher *dry*, had to alienate by degrees his whole worldly Possessions, down almost to the indispensable, or inexpressibles; and die at last in the Paris Hôtel-Dieu; glad that it was not on the street. So that he has, indeed, given a sort of bastard royal life to little Jeanne, and her little brother; but not the smallest earthly provender to keep it in. The mother, in her extremity, forms the wonderfullest connections; and little Jeanne, and her little brother, go out into the highways to beg.

A charitable Countess Boulainvilliers, struck with the little bright-eyed tatterdemalion from the carriage-window, picks her up; has her scoured, clothed; and rears her, in her fluctuating miscellaneous way, to be, about the age of twenty, a nondescript of Mantuamaker, Soubrette, Court-beggar, Fine-lady, Abigail, and Scion-of-Royalty. Sad combination of trades! The Court, after infinite soliciting, puts one off with a hungry dole of little more than thirty pounds a-year. Nay, the audacious Count Boulainvilliers dares, with what purposes he knows best, to offer some suspicious presents! Whereupon his good Countess, especially as Mantuamaking languishes, thinks it could not but be fit to go down to Bar-sur-Aube; and there see whether no fractions of that alienated Fontette Property, held perhaps on insecure tenure, may, by terror or cunning, be recoverable. Burning her paper patterns, pocketing her pension till more come, Mademoiselle Jeanne sallies out thither, in her twenty-third year.

Nourished in this singular way, alternating between saloon and kitchen-table, with the loftiest of pretensions, meanest of possessions, our poor High and Puissant Mantuamaker has realized for herself a "face not beautiful, yet with a certain piquancy;" dark hair, blue eyes; and a character, which the present Writer, a determined student of human nature, declares to be undecipherable. Let the Psychologists try it! Jeanne de-Saint-Remi de Valois de France actually lived, and worked, and was: she has even published, at various times, three considerable Volumes of Autobiography, with loose Leaves (in Courts of Justice) of unknown number; wherein he that runs may read,—but not understand. Strange Volumes! more like the screeching of distracted night-birds (suddenly disturbed by the torch of Police-Fowlers), than the articulate utterance of a rational unfeathered biped. Cheerfully admitting these statements to be all lies; we ask, How any mortal could, or should, *so* lie?

The Psychologists, however, commit one sore mistake; that of searching, in every character named human, for something like a conscience. Being mere contemplative recluses, for most part, and feeling that Morality is the heart of Life, they judge that with all the world it is so. Nevertheless, as practical men are aware, Life can go on in excellent vigor, without crotchet of that kind. What is the essence of Life? Volition? Go deeper down, you find a much more universal root and characteristic: Digestion. While Digestion lasts, Life cannot, in philosophical language, be said to be extinct: and Digestion will give rise to Volitions enough; at any rate, to Desires and attempts, which may pass for such. He who looks neither before nor after, any farther than the Larder and Stateroom, which latter is properly the finest compartment of the Larder, will need no World-theory, Creed as it is called, or Scheme of Duties; lightly leaving the world to wag as it likes with any theory or none, his grand object is a theory and practice of ways and means. Not goodness or badness is the type of him: only shiftiness or shiftlessness.

And now, disburdened of this obstruction, let the Psychologists consider it under a bolder view. Consider the brisk Jeanne de Saint-Remi de Saint-Shifty as a Spark of vehement Life, not developed into Will of any kind, yet fully into Desires of all kinds, and cast into such a Life-element as we have seen. Vanity and Hunger; a Princess of the Blood, yet whose father had sold his inexpressibles; uncertain whether fosterdaughter of a fond Countess, with hopes skyhigh, or supernumerary Soubrette; with not enough of mantuamaking: in a word, *Gigmanity disgigged;* one of the saddest, pitiable, unpitied predicaments of man! She is of that light unreflecting class, of that light unreflecting sex *varium semper et mutabile*. And then her Fine-ladyism though a purseless one: capricious, coquettish, and with all the finer sensibilities of the heart; now in the rackets, now in the sullens; vivid in contradictory resolves; laughing, weeping, without reason, — though these acts are said to be signs of reason. Consider too, how she has had to work her way, all along, by flattery and cajolery; wheedling, eavesdropping, namby-pambying: how she needs wages, and knows no other productive trades. Thought can hardly be said to exist in her: only Perception and Device. With an understanding lynx-eyed for the surface of things, but which pierces beyond the surface of nothing; every individual thing (for she has never seized the heart of it) turns up a new face to her every new day, and seems a thing changed, a different thing. Thus sits, or rather vehemently bobs and hovers her vehement mind, in the middle of a boundless many-dancing whirlpool of gilt-shreds, paper-clippings, and windfalls, — to which the revolving chaos of my Uncle Toby's Smoke-jack was solidity and regularity. Reader! thou for thy sins must have met with such fair Irrationals; fascinating, with their lively eyes, with their quick snappish fancies; distinguished in the higher circles, in Fashion, even in Literature: they hum and buzz there, on graceful film-wings; — searching, nevertheless, with the wonderfullest skill, for honey; "*un*tamable as flies!"

Wonderfullest skill for honey, we say; and, pray, mark that, as regards this Countess de Saint-Shifty.

Her instinct-of-genius is prodigious; her appetite fierce. In any foraging speculation of the private kind, she, unthinking as you call her, will be worth a hundred thinkers. And so of such untamable flies the untamablest, Mademoiselle Jeanne, is now buzzing down, in the Bar-sur-Aube Diligence; to inspect the honey-jars of Fontette; and see and smell whether there be any flaws in them.

Alas, at Fontette, we can, with sensibility, behold straw-roofs we were nursed under; farmers courteously offer cooked milk, and other country messes: but no soul will part with his Landed Property, for which, though cheap, he declares hard money was paid. The honey-jars are all close, then? — However, a certain Monsieur de Lamotte, a tall Gendarme, home on furlough from Lunéville, is now at Bar; pays us attentions; becomes quite particular in his attentions, — for we have a face "with a certain piquancy," the liveliest glib-snappish tongue, the liveliest kittenish manner (not yet hardened into *cat*-hood), with thirty pounds a-year, and prospects. M. de Lamotte, indeed, is as yet only a private sentinel; but then a private sentinel in the *Gendarmes*: and did not his father die fighting "at the head of his company," at Minden? Why not in virtue of our own Countesship dub him too Count; by left-hand collateralism, get him advanced? — Finished before the furlough is done! The untamablest of flies has again buzzed off; in wedlock with M. de Lamotte; if not to get honey, yet to escape spiders; and so lies in garrison at Lunéville, amid coquetries and hysterics, in Gigmanity disgigged, — disconsolate enough.

At the end of four long years (too long), M. de Lamotte, or call him now *Count* de Lamotte, sees good to lay down his fighting-gear (unhappily still only the musket), and become what is by certain moderns called "a Civilian:" not a Civil-Law Doctor; merely a Citizen, one who does not live by being killed. Alas! cold eclipse has all along hung over the Lamotte household. Countess Boulainvilliers, it is true, writes in the most feeling manner; but then the Royal Finances are so deranged! Without personal pressing solicitation, on the spot, no Court-solicitor, were his pension the meagrest, can hope to better it. At Lunéville the sun, indeed, shines; and there is a kind of Life; but only an Un-Parisian, half or quarter Life; the very tradesmen grow clamorous, and no cunningly devised fable, ready-money alone will appease them. Commandant Marquis d'Autichamp agrees with Madame Boulainvilliers that a journey to Paris were the project; whither, also, he himself is just going. Perfidious Commandant Marquis! His plan is seen through: he dares to presume to make love to a Scion-of-Royalty; or to hint that he could dare to presume to do it! Whereupon, indignant Count de Lamotte, as we said, throws up his commission, and down his fire-arms, without further delay. The King loses a tall private sentinel; the World has a new black-leg: and Monsieur and Madame de Lamotte take places in the Diligence for Strasburg.

Good Fostermother Boulainvilliers, however, is no longer at Strasburg: she is forward at the Archiepiscopal Palace in Saverne; on a visit there, to his Eminence

Cardinal Commendator, Grand-Almoner Archbishop Prince Louis de Rohan! Thus, then, has Destiny at last brought it about. Thus, after long wanderings, on paths so far separate, has the time come, in this late year 1783, when, of all the nine hundred millions of the Earth's denizens, these preappointed Two behold each other!

The foolish Cardinal, since no sublunary means, not even bribing of the Trianon Concierge, will serve, has taken to the superlunary: he is here, with his fixed-idea and volcanic vaporosity darkening, under Cagliostro's management, into thicker and thicker opaque, — of the Black-Art itself. To the glance of hungry genius, Cardinal and Cagliostro could not but have meaning. A flush of astonishment, a sigh over boundless wealth (for the mountains of debt lie invisible) in the hands of boundless Stupidity; some vague looming of indefinite hope: all this one can well fancy. But alas, what, to a high plush Cardinal, is a now insolvent Scion-of-Royalty, —though with a face of some piquancy? The good Fostermother's visit, in any case, can last but three days; then, amid old namby-pambyings, with effusions of the nobler sensibilities and tears of pity at least for one's self, Countess de Lamotte, and husband, must off with her to Paris, and new possibilities at Court. Only when the sky again darkens, can this vague looming from Saverne look out, by fits, as a cheering weather-sign.

CHAPTER VI.

WILL THE TWO FIXED-IDEAS UNITE?

HOWEVER, the sky, according to custom, is not long in darkening again. The King's finances, we repeat, are in so distracted a state! No D'Ormesson, no Joly de Fleury, wearied with milking the already dry, will increase that scandalous Thirty Pounds of a Scion-of-Royalty by a single doit. Calonne himself, who has a willing ear and encouraging word for all mortals whatsoever, only with difficulty, and by aid of Madame of France, raises it to some still miserable Sixty-five. Worst of all, the good Fostermother Boulainvilliers, in few months, suddenly dies: the wretched widower, sitting there, with his white handkerchief, to receive condolences, with closed shutters, mortuary tapestries, and sepulchral cressets burning (which, however, the instant the condolences are gone, he blows out, to save oil), has the audacity again, amid crocodile tears, to — drop hints! Nay more, he, wretched man in all senses, abridges the Lamotte table; will besiege virtue both in the positive and negative way. The Lamottes, wintry as the world looks, cannot be gone too soon.

As to Lamotte the husband, he, for shelter against much, decisively dives down to the " subterranean shades of Rascaldom;" gambles, swindles; can hope to live, miscellaneously, if not by the Grace of God, yet by the Oversight of the Devil, — for a time. Lamotte the wife also makes her packages: and waving the unseductive Count Boulainvillier Save-all a disdainful farewell, removes to the *Belle Image* in Versailles; there within wind of Court, in attic apartments, on poor water-gruel board, resolves to await what can betide. So much, in few months of this fateful year, 1783, has come and gone.

Poor Jeanne de Saint-Remi de Lamotte Valois, Ex-Mantuamaker, Scion-of-Royalty! What eye, looking into those bare attic apartments and water-gruel platters of the *Belle Image*, but must, in spite of itself, grow dim with almost a kind of tear for thee! There thou art, with thy quick lively glances, face of a certain piquancy, thy gossamer untamable character, snappish sallies, glib all-managing tongue; thy whole incarnated, garmented, and so sharply appetent "spark of Life;" cast down alive into this World, without vote of thine (for the Elective Franchises have not yet got that length); and wouldst so fain live there. Paying scot-and-lot; providing, or fresh-scouring silk court-dresses; "always keeping a gig!" Thou must hawk and shark to and fro, from anteroom to anteroom; become a kind of terror to all men in place, and women that influence such; dance not light Ionic measures, but attendance merely; have weepings, thanksgiving effusions, aulic, almost forensic, eloquence: perhaps eke out thy thin livelihood by some coquetries, in the small way; — and so, most poverty-stricken, cold-blighted, yet with young keen blood struggling against it, spin forward thy unequal feeble thread, which the Atropos-scissors will soon clip!

Surely now, if ever, were that vague looming from Saverne welcome, as a weather-sign. How doubly welcome is his plush Eminence's personal arrival;—for with the earliest spring he has come in person, as he periodically does; vaporific, driven by his fixed-idea.

Genius, of the mechanical practical kind, what is it but a bringing together of two Forces that fit each other, that will give birth to a third? Ever, from Tubalcain's time, Iron lay ready hammered; Water, also, was boiling and bursting; nevertheless, for want of a genius, there was as yet no Steam-engine. In his Eminence Prince Louis, in that huge, restless, incoherent Being of his, depend on it, brave Countess, there are Forces deep, manifold; nay, a fixed-idea concentrates the whole huge Incoherence as it were into one Force: cannot the eye of genius discover its *fellow?*

Communing much with the Court *valetaille*, our brave Countess has more than once heard talk of Boehmer, of his Necklace, and threatened death by water; in the course of gossiping and tattling, this topic from time to time emerges; is commented upon with empty laughter, — as if there lay no farther meaning in it. To the common eye there is indeed none: but to the eye of genius? In some moment of inspiration, the question rises on our brave Lamotte: Were not *this*, of all extant Forces, the cognate one that would unite with Eminence Rohan's? Great moment, light-beaming, fire-flashing; like birth of Minerva; like all moments of Creation! Fancy how pulse and breath flutter, almost stop, in the greatness: the great not Divine Idea, the great Diabolic Idea, is too big for her. — Thought (how often must we repeat it?) rules the world. Fire and, in a less degree, Frost; Earth and Sea (for what is your swiftest ship, or steamship, but a *Thought* — embodied in wood?); Reformed Parliaments, rise and ruin of Nations, — sale of Diamonds: all things obey Thought. Countess de Saint-Remi de Lamotte, by power of Thought, is now a made woman. With force of genius she represses, crushes deep down, her Undivine Idea; bends all her faculty to realize it. Prepare thyself, Reader, for a series of the most surprising Dramatic Representations ever exhibited on any stage.

We hear tell of Dramatists, and scenic illusion how "natural," how illusive it was: if the spectator, for some half-moment, can half-deceive himself into the belief that it was real, he departs doubly content. With all which, and much more of the like, I have no quarrel. But what must be thought of the Female Dramatist who, for eighteen long months, can exhibit the beautifullest Fata-morgana to a plush Cardinal, wide awake, with fifty years on his head; and so lap him in her scenic illusion that he never doubts but it is all firm earth, and the pasteboard Coulisse-trees are producing Hesperides apples? Could Madame de Lamotte, then, have written a *Hamlet?* I conjecture, not. More goes to the writing of a *Hamlet* than completest "imitation" of all characters and things in this Earth; there goes, before and beyond all, the rarest *understanding* of these, insight into their hidden essences and harmonies. Erasmus's Ape, as is known in Literary History, sat by while its Master was shaving, and " imitated " every point of the process; but its own foolish beard grew never the smoother.

As in looking at a finished Drama, it were nowise meet that the spectator first of all got behind the scenes, and saw the burnt-corks, brayed-resin, thunder-barrels, and withered hunger-bitten men and women, of which such heroic work was made: so here with the reader. A peep into the side-scenes shall be granted him, from time to time. But, on the whole, repress, O reader, that too insatiable scientific curiosity of thine; let thy *æsthetic* feeling first have play; and witness what a Prospero's-grotto poor Eminence Rohan is led into, to be pleased he knows not why.

Survey first what we might call the stage-lights, orchestra, general structure of the theatre, mood and condition of the audience. The theatre is the World, with its restless business and madness; near at hand rise the royal Domes of Versailles, mystery around them, and as background the memory of a thousand years. By the side of the River Seine walks, haggard, wasted, a Joaillier-Bijoutier de la Reine, with Necklace in his pocket. The audience is a drunk Christopher Sly in the fittest humor. A fixed-idea, driving him headlong over steep places, like that of the Gadarenes' Swine, has produced a deceptibility, as of desperation, that will clutch at straws. Understand one other word; Cagliostro is prophesying to him! The Quack of Quacks has now for years had him in leading. Transmitting "predictions in cipher;" questioning, before Hieroglyphic Screens, Columbs in a state of innocence, for elixirs of life, and philosopher's stone; unveiling, in fuliginous clear-obscure, an imaginary majesty of Nature; he isolates him more and more from all unpossessed men. Was it not enough that poor Rohan had become a dissolute, somnolent-violent, ever-vapory Mud-volcano; but black Egyptian magic must be laid on him!

If perhaps, too, our Countess de Lamotte, with her blandishments —? For though not beautiful, she "has a certain piquancy" *et cetera!* — Enough, his poor Eminence sits in the fittest place, in the fittest mood: a newly-awakened Christopher Sly; and with his "small ale," too, beside him. Touch, only, the lights with fire-tipt rod; and let the orchestra, soft-warbling, strike up their fara-lara fiddle-diddle-dee!

CHAPTER VII.

MARIE-ANTOINETTE.

Such a soft-warbling fara-lara was it to his Eminence, when, in early January of the year 1784, our Countess first, mysteriously, and under seal of sworn secrecy, hinted to him that, with her winning tongue and great
5 talent as Anecdotic Historian, she had worked a passage to the ear of Queen's Majesty itself. Gods! dost *thou* bring with thee airs from Heaven? Is thy face yet radiant with some reflex of that Brightness beyond bright?—Men with fixed-idea are not as other men.
10 To listen to a plain varnished tale, such as your Dramatist can fashion; to ponder the words; to snuff them up, as Ephraim did the east-wind, and grow flatulent and drunk with them: what else could poor Eminence do? His poor somnolent, so swift-rocked soul feels a new ele-
15 ment infused into it; turbid resinous light, wide-coruscating, glares over the waste of his imagination. Is he interested in the mysterious tidings? Hope has seized them; there is in the world nothing else that interests him.

20   The secret friendship of Queens is not a thing to be let sleep: ever new Palace Interviews occur;—yet in deepest privacy; for how should her Majesty awaken so

many tongues of Principalities and Nobilities, male and female, that spitefully watch her? Above all, however, "on the 2d of February," that day of "the Procession of blue Ribands," much was spoken of: somewhat, too, of Monseigneur de Rohan!—Poor Monseigneur, hadst thou *three* long ears, thou'dst hear her.

But will she not, perhaps, in some future priceless Interview, speak a good word for thee? Thyself shalt speak it, happy Eminence; at least, write it: our tutelary Countess will be the bearer!—On the 21st of March goes off that long exculpatory imploratory Letter: it is the first Letter that went off from Cardinal to Queen; to be followed, in time, by "above two hundred others;" which are graciously answered by verbal Messages, nay at length by Royal Autographs on gilt paper,—the whole delivered by our tutelary Countess. The tutelary Countess comes and goes, fetching and carrying; with the gravity of a Roman Augur, inspects those extraordinary chicken-bowels, and draws prognostics from them. Things are in fair train: the Dauphiness took some offence at Monseigneur, but the Queen has nigh forgotten it. No inexorable Queen; ah no! So good, so free, light-hearted; only sore beset with malicious Polignacs and others;—at times, also, short of money.

Marie Antoinette, as the reader well knows, has been much blamed for want of Etiquette. Even now, when the other accusations against her have sunk down to oblivion and the Father of Lies, this of wanting Etiquette survives her;—in the Castle of Ham, at this hour, M. de Polignac and Company may be wringing their hands, not without an oblique glance at *her* for bringing them thither. She indeed discarded Etiquette; once, when her carriage broke down, she even entered a hackney-coach. She would walk, too, at Trianon, in mere straw-hat, and perhaps muslin gown! Hence, the Knot of Etiquette being loosed, the Frame of Society broke up; and those astonishing "Horrors of the French Revolution" supervened. On what Damocles' hairs must the judgment-sword hang over this distracted Earth? Thus, however, it was that Tenterden Steeple brought an influx of the Atlantic on us, and so Godwin Sands. Thus, too, might it be that because Father Noah took the liberty of, say, rinsing out his wine-vat, his Ark was floated off, and a world drowned. — Beautiful Highborn that wert so foully hurled low! For, if thy Being came to thee out of old Hapsburg Dynasties, came it not also (like my own) out of Heaven? *Sunt lachrymæ rerum, et mentem mortalia tangunt.* Oh, is there a man's heart that thinks, without pity, of those long months and years of slow-wasting ignominy; — of thy birth, soft-cradled in Imperial Schönbrunn, the winds of heaven not to visit thy face too roughly, thy foot to light on softness, thy eye on splendor; and then of thy Death or hundred Deaths, to which the Guillotine and Fouquier Tinville's judgment-bar was but the merciful end? Look *there*, O man born of woman! The bloom of that fair face is wasted, the hair is gray with care; the brightness of those eyes is quenched, their lids hang drooping, the face is stony pale as of one living in death. Mean weeds, which her own hand has mended, attire the Queen of the World. The death-hurdle, where thou sittest pale, motionless, which only curses environ, has to stop: a people, drunk with vengeance, will drink it again in full draught, looking at thee there. Far as the eye reaches, a multitudinous sea of maniac heads; the air deaf with their triumph-yell! The Living-dead must shudder with yet one other pang; her startled blood yet again suffuses with the hue of agony that pale face, which she hides with her hands. There is then *no* heart to say, God pity thee? Oh think not of these; think of HIM whom thou worshippest, the Crucified,— who also treading the wine-press *alone*, fronted sorrow still deeper; and triumphed over it, and made it holy; and built of it a "Sanctuary of Sorrow," for thee and all the wretched! Thy path of thorns is nigh ended. One long last look at the Tuileries, where thy step was once so light,—where thy children shall not dwell. The head is on the block; the axe rushes—Dumb lies the World; that wild-yelling World, and all its madness, is behind thee.

Beautiful Highborn that wert so foully hurled low! Rest yet in thy innocent gracefully heedless seclusion, unintruded on by *me*, while rude hands have not yet desecrated it. Be the curtains, that shroud-in (if for the last time on this Earth) a Royal Life, still sacred to me. *Thy* fault, in the French Revolution, was that thou wert the Symbol of the Sin and Misery of a thousand years; that with Saint-Bartholomews, and Jacqueries, with Gabelles, and Dragonades, and Parcs-aux-cerfs, the heart of mankind was filled full, — and foamed over, into all-involving madness. To no Napoleon, to no Cromwell wert thou wedded : such sit not in the highest rank, of themselves ; are raised on high by the shaking and confounding of all the ranks ! As poor peasants, how happy, worthy had ye two been ! But by evil destiny ye were made a King and Queen of ; and so both once more — are become an astonishment and a by-word to all times.

CHAPTER VIII.

THE TWO FIXED-IDEAS WILL UNITE.

"COUNTESS DE LAMOTTE, then, had penetrated into the confidence of the Queen? Those gilt-paper Autographs were actually written by the Queen?" Reader, forget not to repress that too insatiable scientific curiosity of thine! What I know is, that a certain Villette-de-Rétaux, with military whiskers, denizen of Rascaldom, comrade there of Monsieur le Comte, is skilful in imitating hands. Certain it is also, that Madame la Comtesse has penetrated to the Trianon — Doorkeeper's. Nay, as Campan herself must admit, she has met, "at a Man-midwife's in Versailles," with worthy Queen's-valet Lesclaux, — or Desclos, for there is no uniformity in it. With these, or the like of these, she in the back-parlor of the Palace itself (if late enough), may pick a merry-thought, sip the foam from a glass of Champagne. No farther seek her honors to disclose, for the present; or anatomically dissect, as we said, those extraordinary chicken-bowels, from which *she*, and she alone, can read Decrees of Fate, and also realize them.

Sceptic, seest thou his Eminence waiting there, in the moonlight; hovering to and fro on the back terrace, till she come out — from the ineffable Interview? He is close muffled; walks restlessly observant; shy also, and courting the shade. She comes: up closer with thy capote, O Eminence, down with thy broadbrim; for she has an escort! 'Tis but the good Monsieur Queen's-valet Lesclaux: and now he is sent back again, as no longer needful. Mark him, Monseigneur, nevertheless; thou wilt see him yet another time. Monseigneur marks little: his heart is in the ineffable Interview, in the gilt-paper Autograph alone. — Queen's-valet Lesclaux? Methinks he has much the stature of Villette, denizen of Rascaldom! Impossible!

How our Countess managed with Cagliostro? Cagliostro, gone from Strasburg, is as yet far distant, winging his way through dim Space; will not be here for months: only his "predictions in cipher" are here. Here or there, however, Cagliostro, to our Countess, can be useful. At a glance, the eye of genius has descried him to be a bottomless slough of falsity, vanity, gulosity and thick-eyed stupidity: of foulest material, but of fattest; — fit compost for the Plant she is rearing. Him who has deceived all Europe she can undertake to deceive. His Columbs, demonic Masonries, Egyptian Elixirs, what is all this to the light-giggling exclusively practical Lamotte? It runs off from her, as all speculation, good, bad and indifferent, has always done, "like water from one in wax-cloth dress." With the lips meanwhile she can honor it; Oil of Flattery, the best patent antifriction known, subdues all irregularities whatsoever.

On Cagliostro, again, on his side, a certain uneasy

feeling might, for moments, intrude itself; the raven loves not ravens. But what can he do? Nay, she is partly playing *his* game: can he not spill her full cup yet, at the right season, and pack her out of doors? Oftenest in their joyous orgies, this light fascinating Countess, — who perhaps has a design on *his* heart, seems to him but one other of those light *Papiliones*, who have fluttered round him in all climates; whom with grim muzzle he has snapt by the thousand.

Thus, what with light fascinating Countess, what with Quack of Quacks, poor Eminence de Rohan lies safe; his mud-volcano placidly simmering in thick Egyptian haze: withdrawn from all the world. Moving figures, as of men, he sees; takes not the trouble to look at. Court-cousins rally him; are answered in silence; or, if it go too far, in mud-explosions terrifico-absurd. Court-cousins and all mankind are unreal shadows merely; Queen's favor the only substance.

Nevertheless, the World, on its side too, has an existence; lies not idle in these days. It has got its Versailles Treaty signed, long months ago; and the plenipotentiaries all home again, for votes of thanks. Paris, London and other great Cities and small, are working, intriguing; dying, being born. There, in the Rue Taranne, for instance, the once noisy Denis Diderot has fallen silent enough. Here also, in Bolt Court, old Samuel Johnson, like an over-wearied Giant, must lie down, and slumber without dream; — the rattling of carriages and wains, and all the world's din and business rolling by, as ever, from of old. — Sieur Boehmer, however, has not yet drowned himself in the Seine; only walks haggard, wasted, purposing to do it.

News (by the merest accident in the world) reach Sieur Boehmer, of Madame's new favor with her Majesty! Men will do much before they drown. Sieur Boehmer's Necklace is on Madame's table, his guttural-nasal rhetoric in her ear: he will abate many a pound and penny of the first just price; he will give cheerfully a thousand Louis-d'or, as *cadeau*, to the generous Scion-of-Royalty that shall persuade her Majesty. The man's importunities grow quite annoying to our Countess; who, in her glib way, satirically prattles how she has been bored, — to Monseigneur, among others.

Dozing on down cushions, far inwards, with soft ministering Hebes, and luxurious appliances; with ranked Heyducs, and a *Valetaille* innumerable, that shut out the prose-world and its discord: thus lies Monseigneur, in enchanted dream. Can he, even in sleep, forget his tutelary Countess, and her service? By the delicatest presents he alleviates her distresses, most undeserved. Nay, once or twice, gilt Autographs, from a Queen, — with whom he is evidently rising to unknown heights in favor, — have done Monseigneur the honor to make him *her* Majesty's Grand Almoner, when the case was pressing. Monseigneur, we say, has had the honor to disburse charitable cash, on her Majesty's behalf, to this or the other distressed deserving object: say only to the length of a few thousand pounds, advanced from his own funds; — her Majesty being at the moment so poor, and charity a thing that will not wait. Always Madame, good, foolish, gadding creature, takes charge of delivering the money. — Madame can descend from her attics, in the *Belle Image;* and feel the smiles of Nature and Fortune, a little; so bounteous has the Queen's Majesty been.

To Monseigneur the power of money over highest female hearts had never been incredible. Presents have, many times, worked wonders. But then, O Heavens, *what* present? Scarcely were the Cloud-Compeller himself, all coined into new Louis-d'or, worthy to alight in such a lap. Loans, charitable disbursements, however, as we see, are permissible; these, by defect of payment, may become presents. In the vortex of his Eminence's day-dreams, lumbering multiform slowly round, this of importunate Boehmer and his Necklace, from time to time, turns up. Is the Queen's Majesty at heart desirous of it; but again, at the moment, too poor? Our tutelary Countess answers vaguely, mysteriously; — confesses, at last, under oath of secrecy, her own private suspicion that the Queen wants this same Necklace, of all things; but dare not, for a stingy husband, buy it. She, the Countess de Lamotte, will look farther into the matter; and, if aught serviceable to his Eminence can be suggested, in a good way suggest it, in the proper quarter.

Walk warily, Countess de Lamotte; for now, with thickening breath, thou approachest the moment of moments! Principalities and Powers, *Parlement, Grand*

Chambre and *Tournelle*, with all their whips and gibbet-wheels; the very Crack of Doom hangs over thee, if thou trip. Forward, with nerve of iron, on shoes of felt; *like* a Treasure-digger, in silence, looking neither to the right nor left, — where yawn abysses deep as the Pool, and all Pandemonium hovers, eager to rend thee into rags!

CHAPTER IX.

PARK OF VERSAILLES.

Or will the reader incline rather, taking the other and sunny side of the matter, to enter that Lamottic Circean theatrical establishment of Monseigneur de Rohan; and see there how, under the best of Dramaturgists, Melodrama with sweeping pall flits past him; while the enchanted Diamond fruit is gradually ripening, to fall by a shake?

The 28th of July, of this same momentous 1784, has come; and with it the most rapturous tumult into the heart of Monseigneur. Ineffable expectancy stirs-up his whole soul, with the much that lies therein, from its lowest foundations: borne on wild seas to Armida Islands, yet as is fit, through Horror dim-hovering round, he tumultuously rocks. To the Château, to the Park! This night the Queen will meet thee, the Queen herself: so far has our tutelary Countess brought it. What can ministerial impediments, Polignac intrigues, avail against the favor, nay — Heaven and Earth! — perhaps the tenderness of a Queen? She vanishes from amid their meshwork of Etiquette and Cabal; descends from her celestial Zodiac, to thee a shepherd of Latmos. Alas, a white-bearded pursy shepherd, fat and scant of breath! Who can account for the taste of females? But thou, burnish-up thy whole faculties of gallantry, thy fifty-years experience of the sex; this night, or never!— In such unutterable meditations does Monseigneur restlessly spend the day; and long for darkness, yet dread it.

Darkness has at length come. The perpendicular rows of Heyducs, in that Palais or Hôtel de Strasbourg, are all cast horizontal, prostrate in sleep; the very Concierge resupine, with open mouth, audibly drinks-in nepenthe; when Monseigneur, "in blue great-coat, with slouched hat, issues softly, with his henchman Planta of the Grisons, to the Park of Versailles. Planta must loiter invisible in the distance; Slouched-hat will wait here, among the leafy thickets; till our tutelary Countess, "in black domino," announce the moment, which surely must be near.

The night is of the darkest for the season; no Moon; warm, slumbering July, in motionless clouds, drops fatness over the Earth. The very stars from the Zenith see not Monseigneur; see only his and the world's cloud-covering, fringed with twilight in the far North. Midnight, telling itself forth from these shadowy Palace Domes? All the steeples of Versailles, the villages around, with metal tongue, and huge Paris itself dull-droning, answer drowsily, Yes! Sleep rules this Hemisphere of the World. From Arctic to Antarctic, the Life of our Earth lies all, in long swaths, or rows (like those rows of Heyducs and snoring Concierge), successively mown down, from vertical to horizontal, by Sleep! Rather curious to consider.

The flowers are all asleep in Little Trianon, the roses folded-in for the night; but the Rose of Roses still wakes. O wondrous Earth! O doubly wondrous Park of Versailles, with Little and Great Trianon,— and a scarce-breathing Monseigneur! Ye Hydraulics of Lenôtre. that also slumber, with stop-cocks, in your deep leaden chambers, babble not of *him*, when ye arise. Ye odorous balm-shrubs, huge spectral Cedars, thou sacred Boscage of Hornbeam, ye dim Pavilions of the Peerless, whisper not! Moon, lie silent, hidden in thy vacant cave; no star look down: let neither Heaven nor Hell peep through the blanket of the Night, to cry, Hold, Hold! — The Black Domino? Ha! Yes! — With stouter step than might have been expected, Monseigneur is under way; the Black Domino had only to whisper, low and eager: "In the Hornbeam Arbor!" And now, Cardinal, O now! — Yes, there hovers the white Celestial; "in white robe of *linon moucheté*," finer than moonshine; a Juno by her bearing: there, in that bosket! Monseigneur, down on thy knees; never can red breeches be better wasted. Oh, he would kiss the royal shoe-tie, or its shadow if there were one: not words; only broken gaspings, murmuring prostrations, eloquently speak his meaning. But, ah, behold! Our tutelary Black Domino, in haste, with vehement whisper: "*On vient.*" The white Juno drops a fairest Rose, with these ever-memorable words, "*Vous savez ce que cela veut dire*, You know what that means;" vanishes in the thickets, the Black Domino hurrying her with eager whisper of "*Vite, vite*, Away, away!" for the sound of footsteps (doubtless from Madame, and Madame d'Artois, unwelcome sisters that they are!) is approaching fast. Monseigneur picks up his Rose; runs as for the King's plate, almost overturns poor Planta, whose laugh assures him that all is safe.

O Ixion de Rohan, happiest mortal of this world, since the first Ixion, of deathless memory, — who nevertheless, in that cloud-embrace, begat strange Centaurs! Thou art Prime Minister of France without peradventure: is not this the Rose of Royalty, worthy to become ottar of roses, and yield perfume forever? How *thou*, of all people, wilt contrive to govern France, in these very peculiar times — But that is little to the matter. There, doubtless, is thy Rose (which methinks, it were well to have a Box or Casket made for): nay, was there not in the dulcet of thy Juno's "*Vous savez*" a kind of trepidation, a quaver, — as of still deeper meanings!

Reader, there is hitherto no item of this miracle that is not historically proved and *true.* — In distracted black-magical phantasmagory, adumbrations of yet higher and highest Dalliances hover stupendous in the background: whereof your Georgels, and Campans, and other official characters *can* take no notice! There, in distracted black-magical phantasmagory, let these hover. The truth of them for us is that they do so hover. The truth of them in itself is known only to three persons: Dame self-styled Countess de Lamotte; the Devil; and Philippe Egalité, — who furnished money and facts for the Lamotte *Memoirs,* and, before guillotinement, begat the present King of the French.

Enough that Ixion de Rohan, lapsed almost into deliquium, by such sober certainty of waking bliss, is the happiest of all men; and his tutelary Countess the dearest of all women, save one only. On the 25th of August (so strong still are those villanous Drawing-room cabals) he goes, weeping, but submissive, by order of a gilt Autograph, home to Saverne; till farther dignities can be matured for him. He carries his Rose, now considerably faded, in a Casket of fit price; may, if he so please, perpetuate it as *pot-pourri*. He names a favorite walk in his Archiepiscopal pleasure-grounds, *Promenade de la Rose;* there let him court digestion, and loyally somnambulate till called for.

I notice it as a coincidence in chronology, that, few days after this date, the Demoiselle (or even, for the last month, Baroness) Gay d'Oliva began to find Countess de Lamotte "not at home," in her fine Paris hotel, in her fine Charonne country-house; and went no more, with Villette, and such pleasant dinner-guests, and her, to see Beaumarchais' *Mariage de Figaro* running its hundred nights.

CHAPTER X.

BEHIND THE SCENES.

"THE Queen?" Good reader, *thou* surely art not a Partridge the Schoolmaster or a Monseigneur de Rohan, to mistake the stage for a reality!—"But who this Demoiselle d'Oliva was?" Reader, let us remark rather how the labors of our Dramaturgic Countess are increasing.

New actors I see on the scene; not one of whom shall guess what the other is doing; or, indeed, know rightly what himself is doing. For example, cannot Messieurs de Lamotte and Villette, of Rascaldom, like Nisus and Euryalus, take a midnight walk of contemplation, with "footsteps of Madame and Madame d'Artois" (since all footsteps are much the same), without offence to any one? A Queen's Similitude can believe that a Queen's Self, for frolic's sake, is looking at her through the thickets; a terrestrial Cardinal can kiss with devotion a celestial Queen's slipper, or Queen's Similitude's slipper,—and no one but a Black Domino the wiser. All these shall follow each his precalculated course; for their inward mechanism is known, and fit wires hook themselves on this. To Two only is a clear belief vouchsafed: to Monseigneur, a clear belief founded on stupidity: to the great creative Dramaturgist, sitting at the heart of the whole mystery, a clear belief founded on completest insight. Great creative Dramaturgist! How, like Schiller, "by union of the Possible with the Necessarily existing, she brings out the" — Eighty thousand Pounds! Don Aranda, with his triple-sealed missives and hoodwinked secretaries, bragged justly that he cut down the Jesuits in one day: but here, without ministerial salary, or King's favor, or any help beyond her own black domino, labors a greater than he. How she advances, stealthily, steadfastly, with Argus eye and ever-ready brain; with nerve of iron, on shoes of felt! O worthy to have intrigued for Jesuitdom, for Pope's Tiara; — to have been Pope Joan thyself, in those old days; and as Arachne of Arachnes, sat in the centre of that stupendous spider-web, which, reaching from Goa to Acapulco, and from Heaven to Hell, overnetted the thoughts and souls of men! — Of which spider-web stray tatters, in favorable dewy mornings, even yet become visible.

The Demoiselle d'Oliva? She is a Parisian Demoiselle of three-and-twenty, tall, blond and beautiful; from unjust guardians, and an evil world, she has had somewhat to suffer.

"In this month of June 1784," says the Demoiselle herself, in her (judicial) Autobiography, "I occupied a small apartment in the Rue du Jour, Quartier St. Eustache. I was not far from the Garden of the Palais-Royal; I had made it my usual promenade." For, indeed, the real God's-truth is, I was a Parisian unfortunate-female, with moderate custom; and one must go where his market lies. "I frequently passed three or four hours of the afternoon there, with some women of my acquaintance, and a little child of four years old, whom I was fond of, whom his parents willingly trusted with me. I even went thither alone, except for him, when other company failed.

"One afternoon, in the month of July following, I was at the Palais-Royal: my whole company, at the moment, was the child I speak of. A tall young man, walking alone, passes several times before me. He was a man I had never seen. He looks at me; he looks fixedly at me. I observe even that always, as he comes near, he slackens his pace, as if to survey me more at leisure. A chair stood vacant; two or three feet from mine. He seats himself there.

"Till this instant, the sight of the young man, his walks, his approaches, his repeated gazings, had made no impression on me. But now when he was sitting so close by, I could not avoid noticing him. His eyes ceased not to wander over all my person. His air becomes earnest, grave. An unquiet curiosity appears to agitate him. He seems to measure my figure, to seize by turns all parts of my physiognomy. — He finds me (but whispers not a syllable of it) tolerably like, both in person and profile; for even the Abbé Georgel says, I was a *belle courtisane*.

"It is time to name this young man: he was the Sieur de Lamotte, styling himself Comte de Lamotte. Who doubts it? He praises 'my feeble charms;' expresses a wish to 'pay his addresses to me.' I, being a lone spinster, know not what to say; think it best in the mean while to retire. Vain precaution! I see him all on a sudden appear in my apartment!"

On his "ninth visit" (for he was always civility itself), he talks of introducing a great Court-lady, by whose means I may even do her Majesty some little secret-service, — the reward of which will be unspeakable. In the dusk of the evening, silks mysteriously rustle: enter the creative Dramaturgist, Dame styled Countess de Lamotte; and so — the too intrusive scientific reader has now, for his punishment, *got* on the wrong-side of that loveliest Transparency; finds nothing but grease-pots, and vapor of expiring wicks!

The Demoiselle Gay d'Oliva may once more sit, or stand, in the Palais-Royal, with such custom as will come. In due time, she shall again, but with breath of Terror, be blown upon; and blown out of France to Brussels.

CHAPTER XI.

THE NECKLACE IS SOLD.

AUTUMN, with its gray moaning winds and coating of red strewn leaves, invites Courtiers to enjoy the charms of Nature; and all business of moment stands still. Countess de Lamotte, while everything is so stagnant, and even Boehmer has locked up his Necklace and his hopes for the season, can drive, with her Count and Euryalus Villette, down to native Bar-sur-Aube; and there (in virtue of a Queen's bounty) show the envious a Scion-of-royalty *re*-grafted; and make them yellower looking on it. A well-varnished chariot, with the Arms of Valois duly painted in bend-sinister; a house gallantly furnished, bodies gallantly attired, — secure them the favorablest reception from all manner of men. The very Duc de Penthièvre (Egalité's father-in-law) welcomes our Lamotte, with that urbanity characteristic of his high station and the old school. Worth, indeed, makes the man, or woman; but "leather" of gig-straps, and "prunella" of gig-lining, first makes it *go*.

The great creative Dramaturgist has thus let down her drop-scene; and only, with a Letter or two to Saverne, or even a visit thither (for it is but a day's drive from Bar), keeps up a due modicum of intermediate instru-

mental music. She needs some pause, in good sooth, to
collect herself a little; for the last act and grand Catas-
trophe is at hand. Two fixed-ideas, Cardinal's and Jeweller's, a negative and a positive, have felt each other;
stimulated now by new hope, are rapidly revolving round
each other, and approximating; like two flames, are
stretching-out long fire-tongues to join and be one.

Boehmer, on his side, is ready with the readiest; as
indeed he has been these four long years. The Countess,
it is true, will have neither part nor lot in that foolish
Cadeau of his, or in the whole foolish Necklace business:
this she has, in plain words, and even not without as-
perity, due to a bore of such magnitude, given him to
know. From her, nevertheless, by cunning inference,
and the merest accident in the world, the sly Joaillier-
Bijoutier has gleaned thus much, that Monseigneur de
Rohan is the man. — Enough! Enough! Madame shall
be no more troubled. Rest there, in hope, thou Necklace of the Devil; but, O Monseigneur, be thy return
speedy!

Alas, the man lives not that would be speedier than
Monseigneur, if he durst. But as yet no gilt Autograph
invites him, permits him; the few gilt Autographs are
all negatory, procrastinating. Cabals of Court; forever
cabals! Nay if it be not for some Necklace, or other such
crotchet or necessity, who knows but he may *never* be
recalled (so fickle is womankind); but forgotten, and
left to rot here, like his Rose, into *pot-pourri?* Our tutelary Countess, too, is shyer in this matter than we ever

saw her. Nevertheless, by intense skilful cross-questioning, he has extorted somewhat; sees partly how it stands. The Queen's Majesty will have her Necklace; for when, in such case, had not woman her way? The Queen's Majesty can even pay for it — by instalments; but then the stingy husband! Once for all, she will not be seen in the business. Now, therefore, Were it, or were it not, permissible to mortal to transact it secretly in her stead? That is the question. If to mortal, then to Monseigneur. Our Countess has even ventured to hint afar off at Monseigneur (kind Countess!) in the proper quarter; but his discretion in regard to money-matters is doubted. Discretion? And I on the *Promenade de la Rose?* — Explode not, O Eminence! Trust will spring of trial; thy hour is coming.

The Lamottes meanwhile have left their farewell card with all the respectable classes of Bar-sur-Aube; our Dramaturgist stands again behind the scenes at Paris. How is it, O Monseigneur, that she is still so shy with thee, in this matter of the Necklace; that she leaves the love-lorn Latmian shepherd to droop, here in lone Saverne, like weeping-ash, in naked winter, on his Promenade of the Rose, with vague commonplace responses that his hour is coming? — By Heaven and Earth! at last, in late January, it is *come*. Behold it, this new gilt Autograph: "To Paris, on a small business of delicacy, which our Countess will explain," — which I already know! To Paris! Horses; postilions; beefeaters!—And so his resuscitated Eminence, all wrapt in furs, in the pleasantest frost (Abbé Georgel says, *un beau froid de Janvier*), over clear-jingling highway rolls rapidly, — borne on the bosom of Dreams.

O Dame de Lamotte, has the enchanted Diamond fruit ripened, then? Hast thou *given* it the little shake, big with unutterable fate? — I? can the Dame justly retort: Who saw me in it? — The reader, therefore, has still Three scenic Exhibitions to look at, by our great Dramaturgist; then the Fourth and last, — by another Author.

To us, reflecting how oftenest the true moving force in human things works hidden underground, it seems small marvel that this month of January 1785, wherein our Countess so little courts the eye of the vulgar historian, should nevertheless have been the busiest of all for her; especially the latter half thereof.

Wisely eschewing matters of Business (which she could never in her life understand), our Countess will personally take no charge of that bargain-making; leaves it all to her Majesty and the gilt Autographs. Assiduous Boehmer nevertheless is in frequent close conference with Monseigneur: the Paris Palais-de-Strasbourg, shut to the rest of men, sees the Joaillier-Bijoutier, with eager official aspect, come and go. The grand difficulty is — must we say it? — her Majesty's wilful whimsicality, unacquaintance with Business. She positively will not write a gilt Autograph, *authorizing* his Eminence to make the bargain; but writes rather, in a pettish manner, that the thing is of no consequence, and can be given up! Thus must the poor Countess dash to and fro, like a weaver's shuttle, between Paris and Versailles; wear her horses and nerves to pieces; nay, sometimes in the hottest haste, wait many hours within call of the Palace, considering what *can* be done (with none but Villette to bear her company), — till the Queen's whim pass.

At length, after furious-driving and conferences enough, on the 29th of January, a middle course is hit on. Cautious Boehmer shall write out, on finest paper, his terms; which are really rather fair: Sixteen hundred thousand livres; to be paid in five equal instalments; the first this day six months; the other four from three months to three months; this is what Court-Jewellers Boehmer and Bassange, on the one part, and Prince Cardinal Commendator Louis de Rohan, on the other part, will stand to; witness their hands. Which written sheet of finest paper our poor Countess must again take charge of, again dash-off with to Versailles; and therefrom, after trouble unspeakable (shared in only by the faithful Villette, of Rascaldom), return with it, bearing this most precious marginal note, "*Bon* — *Marie-Antoinette de France*," in the Autograph-hand! Happy Cardinal! this *thou* shalt keep in the innermost of all thy repositories. Boehmer meanwhile, secret as Death, shall tell no man that he has sold his Necklace; or if much pressed for an actual sight of the same, confess that it is sold to the Favorite Sultana of the Grand Turk for the time being.

Thus, then, do the smoking Lamotte horses at length

get rubbed down, and feel the taste of oats, after midnight; the Lamotte Countess can also gradually sink into needful slumber, perhaps not unbroken by dreams. On the morrow the bargain shall be concluded; next day the Necklace be delivered, on Monseigneur's receipt.

Will the reader, therefore, be pleased to glance at the following two Life-Pictures, Real-Phantasmagories, or whatever we may call them; they are the two first of those Three scenic real-poetic exhibitions, brought about by our **Dramaturgist**: short Exhibitions, but essential ones.

CHAPTER XII.

THE NECKLACE VANISHES.

It is the first day of February; that grand day of Delivery. The Sieur Boehmer is in the Court of the Palais de Strasbourg; his look mysterious-official, and though much emaciated, radiant with enthusiasm. The Seine has missed him; though lean, he will fatten again, and live through new enterprises.

Singular, were we not used to it: the name "Boehmer," as it passes upwards and inwards, lowers all halberts of Heyducs in perpendicular rows: the historical eye beholds him, bowing low, with plenteous smiles, in the plush Saloon of Audience. Will it please Monseigneur, then, to do the *ne-plus-ultra* of Necklaces the honor of looking at it? A piece of Art, which the Universe cannot parallel, shall be parted with (Necessity compels Court-Jewellers) at that ruinously low sum. They, the Court-Jewellers, shall have much ado to weather it; but their work, at least, will find a fit Wearer, and go down to juster posterity. Monseigneur will merely have the condescension to sign this Receipt of Delivery: all the rest, her Highness the Sultana of the Sublime Porte has settled it. — Here the Court-Jeweller, with his joyous though now much-emaciated face, ventures on a faint knowing smile; to which, in the lofty dissolute-serene of Monseigneur's, some twinkle of permission could not but respond. — This is the First of those Three real-poetic Exhibitions, brought about by our Dramaturgist, — with perfect success.

It was said, long afterwards, that Monseigneur should have known, and even that Boehmer should have known, her Highness the Sultana's marginal note, her *"Right — Marie Antoinette of France,"* to be a forgery and mockery: the *"of France"* was fatal to it. Easy talking, easy criticising! But how are two enchanted men to know; two men with a fixed-idea each, a negative and a positive, rushing together to neutralize each other in rapture? — Enough, Monseigneur has the *ne-plus-ultra* of Necklaces, conquered by man's valor and woman's wit; and rolls off with it, in mysterious speed, to Versailles, — triumphant as a Jason with his Golden Fleece.

The Second grand scenic Exhibition by our Dramaturgic Countess occurs in her own apartment at Versailles, so early as the following night. It is a commodious apartment, with alcove; and the alcove has a glass door. Monseigneur enters, — with a follower bearing a mysterious Casket, who carefully deposits it, and then respectfully withdraws. It is the Necklace itself in all its glory! Our tutelary Countess, and Monseigneur, and we, can at leisure admire the queenly Talisman; congratulate ourselves that the painful conquest of it is achieved.

But, hist! A knock, mild but decisive, as from one knocking with authority! Monseigneur and we retire

to our alcove; there from behind our glass screen, observe what passes. Who comes? The door flung open: *de par la Reine!* Behold him, Monseigneur: he enters with grave, respectful, yet official air; worthy Monsieur
5 Queen's-valet Lesclaux, the same who escorted our tutelary Countess, that moonlight night, from the back apartments of Versailles. Said we not, thou wouldst see *him* once more? — Methinks, again, spite of his Queen's-uniform, he has much the features of Villette of
10 Rascaldom! — Rascaldom or Valetdom (for to the blind all colors are the same), he has, with his grave, respectful, yet official air, received the Casket, and its priceless contents; with fit injunction, with fit engagements; and retires bowing low.
15 Thus softly, silently, like a very Dream, flits away our solid Necklace — through the Horn Gate of Dreams!

CHAPTER XIII.

SCENE THIRD: BY DAME DE LAMOTTE.

Now too, in these same days (as he can afterwards prove by affidavit of Landlords) arrives Count Cagliostro himself, from Lyons! No longer by predictions in cipher; but by his living voice, often in rapt communion with the unseen world, " with Caraffe and four candles;" by his greasy prophetic bull-dog face, said to be the " most perfect quack-face of the eighteenth century," can we assure ourselves that all is well; that all will turn "to the glory of Monseigneur, to the good of France, and of mankind," and of Egyptian masonry. " Tokay flows like water;" our charming Countess, with her piquancy of face, is sprightlier than ever; enlivens with the brightest sallies, with the adroitest flatteries to all, those suppers of the gods. O Nights, O Suppers — too good to last! Nay, now also occurs another and Third scenic Exhibition, fitted by its radiance to dispel from Monseigneur's soul the last trace of care.

Why the Queen does not, even yet, openly receive me at Court? Patience, Monseigneur! Thou little knowest those too intricate cabals; and how she still but works at them silently, with royal suppressed fury, like a royal lioness only *delivering* herself from the hunter's toils. Meanwhile, is not thy work done? The Necklace, she rejoices over it; beholds, many times in secret, her Juno-neck mirrored back the lovelier for it, — as our tutelar Countess can testify. Come to-morrow to the *Œil-de-Bœuf;* there see with eyes, in high noon, as already in deep midnight thou hast seen, whether in *her* royal heart there were delay.

Let us stand, then, with Monseigneur, in that *Œil-de-Bœuf*, in the Versailles Palace Gallery; for all well-dressed persons are admitted: there the Loveliest, in pomp of royalty, will walk to mass. The world is all in pelisses and winter furs; cheerful, clear, — with noses tending to blue. A lively many-voiced hum plays fitful, hither and thither: of sledge parties and Court parties; frosty state of the weather; stability of M. de Calonne; Majesty's looks yesterday; — such hum as always, in these sacred Court-spaces, since Louis le Grand made and consecrated them, has, with more or less impetuosity, agitated our common Atmosphere.

Ah, through that long high Gallery what Figures have passed — and vanished! Louvois, — with the Great King, flashing fire-glances on the fugitive; in his red right hand a pair of tongs, which pious Maintenon hardly holds back: Louvois, where art thou? Ye *Maréchaux de France?* Ye unmentionable-women of past generations? Here also was it that rolled and rushed the "sound, absolutely like thunder," of Courtier hosts; in that dark hour when the signal-light in Louis the Fifteenth's chamber-window was blown out; and his ghastly infectious Corpse lay lone, forsaken on its tumbled death-lair, "in the hands of some poor women;" and the Courtier-hosts rushed from the Deep-fallen to hail the New-risen! These too rushed, and passed; and their "sound, absolutely like thunder," became silence. Figures? Men? They are fast-fleeting Shadows; fast chasing each other: it is not a Palace, but a Caravansera. — Monseigneur (with thy too much Tokay overnight)! cease puzzling: here *thou* art, this blessed February day: — the Peerless, will she turn lightly that high head of hers, and glance aside into the *Œil-de-Bœuf*, in passing? Please Heaven, she will. To our tutelary Countess, at least, she promised it; though, alas, so fickle is womankind! —

Hark! Clang of opening doors! She issues, like the Moon in silver brightness, down the Eastern steeps. *La Reine vient!* What a figure! I (with the aid of glasses) discern *her*. O Fairest, Peerless! Let the hum of minor discoursing hush itself wholly; and only one successive rolling peal of *Vive la Reine*, like the movable radiance of a train of fire-works, irradiate her path. — Ye Immortals! She does, she beckons, turns her head this way! — "Does she not?" says Countess de Lamotte. — Versailles, the *Œil-de-Bœuf*, and all men and things are drowned in a Sea of Light; Monseigneur and that high beckoning Head are alone, with each other in the Universe.

O Eminence, what a beatific vision! Enjoy it, blest as the gods; ruminate and re-enjoy it, with full soul: it is the last provided for thee. Too soon, in the course of these six months, shall thy beatific vision, like Mirza's vision, gradually melt away; and only oxen and sheep be grazing in its place; — and thou, as a doomed Nebuchadnezzar, be grazing with them.

"Does she not?" said the Countess de Lamotte. That it is a habit of hers; that hardly a day passes *without* her doing it: this the Countess de Lamotte did not say.

CHAPTER XIV.

THE NECKLACE CANNOT BE PAID.

HERE, then, the specially Dramaturgic labors of Countess de Lamotte may be said to terminate. The rest of her life is Histrionic merely, or Histrionic and Critical; as, indeed, what had all the former part of it been but a *Hypocrisia*, a more or less correct Playing of Parts? O "Mrs. Facing-both-ways" (as old Bunyan said), what a talent hadst thou! No Proteus ever took so many shapes, no Chameleon so often changed color. One thing thou wert to Monseigneur; another thing to Cagliostro, and Villette of Rascaldom; a third thing to the World, in printed *Mémoires;* a fourth thing to Philippe Egalité: all things to all men!

Let her, however, we say, but manage now to *act* her own parts, with proper Histrionic illusion; and, by Critical glosses, give her past Dramaturgy the fit aspect, to Monseigneur and others: this henceforth, and not new Dramaturgy, includes her whole task. Dramatic Scenes, in plenty, will follow of themselves; especially that Fourth and final Scene, spoken of above as by another Author, — by Destiny itself.

For in the Lamotte Theatre, so different from our common Pasteboard one, the Play goes on, even when the Machinist has left it. Strange enough: those Air-images, which from her Magic-lantern she hung out on the empty bosom of Night, have clutched hold of this solid-seeming World (which some call the Material World, as if that made it more a Real one), and will tumble hither and thither the solidest masses there. Yes, reader, so goes it here below. What thou callest a Brain-web, or mere illusive Nothing, *is* it not a web of the Brain; of the Spirit which inhabits the Brain; and which, in this World (rather, as I think, to be named the Spiritual one), very naturally moves and tumbles hither and thither all things it meets with, in Heaven or in Earth? — So too, the Necklace, though we saw it vanish through the Horn Gate of Dreams, and in my opinion man shall never more behold it, — yet its activity ceases not, nor will. For no Act of a man, no Thing (how much less the man himself!) is extinguished when *it* disappears: through considerable times it still visibly works, though done and vanished; I have known a done thing work visibly Three Thousand Years and more: invisibly, unrecognized, all done things work through endless times and years. Such a Hypermagical is this our poor old Real world; which some take upon them to pronounce effete, prosaic! Friend, it is thyself that art all withered up into effete Prose, dead as ashes: know this (I advise thee); and seek passionately, with a passion little short of desperation, to have it remedied.

Meanwhile, what will the feeling heart think to learn that Monseigneur de Rohan, as we prophesied, again experiences the fickleness of a Court; that, notwithstanding the beatific visions, at noon and midnight, the Queen's Majesty, with the light ingratitude of her sex, flies off at a tangent; and, far from ousting his detested and detesting rival, Minister Breteuil, and openly delighting to honor Monseigneur, will hardly vouchsafe him a few gilt Autographs, and those few of the most capricious, suspicious, soul-confusing tenor? What terrifico-absurd explosions, which scarcely Cagliostro, with Caraffe and four candles, can still; how many deep-weighed Humble Petitions, Explanations, Expostulations, penned with fervidest eloquence, with craftiest diplomacy, — all delivered by our tutelar Countess: in vain! — O Cardinal, with what a huge iron mace, like Guy of Warwick's, thou smitest Phantasms in two, which close again, take shape again; and only thrashest the air!

One comfort, however, is that the Queen's Majesty has committed herself. The Rose of Trianon, and what may pertain thereto, lies it not here? That "*Right — Marie Antoinette of France*," too; and the 30th of July, first-instalment-day, coming? She shall be *brought* to terms, good Eminence! Order horses and beef-eaters for Saverne; there, ceasing all written or oral communication, starve her into capitulating. It is the bright May month: his Eminence again somnambulates the *Promenade de la Rose;* but now with grim dry eyes; and, from time to time, terrifically stamping.

But who is this that I see mounted on costliest horse and horse-gear; betting at Newmarket Races; though he can speak no English word, and only some Chevalier O'Niel, some Capuchin Macdermot, from Bar-sur-Aube, interprets his French into the dialect of the Sister Island? Few days ago I observed him walking in Fleet-street, thoughtfully through Temple-Bar;— in deep treaty with Jeweller Jeffreys, with Jeweller Grey, for the sale of Diamonds: such a lot as one may boast of. A tall handsome man; with ex-military whiskers; with a look of troubled gayety, and rascalism: you think it is the Sieur self-styled Count de Lamotte; nay the man himself confesses it! The Diamonds were a present to his Countess,— from the still-bountiful Queen.

Villette too, has he completed his sales at Amsterdam? Him I shall by and by behold; not betting at Newmarket, but drinking wine and ardent spirits in the Taverns of Geneva. Ill-gotten wealth endures not; Rascaldom has no strong-box. Countess de Lamotte, for what a set of cormorant scoundrels hast thou labored, art thou still laboring!

Still laboring, we may say: for as the fatal 30th of July approaches, what is to be looked for but universal Earthquake; Mud-explosion that will blot-out the face of Nature? Methinks, stood I in thy pattens, Dame de Lamotte, I would cut and run. — "Run!" exclaims she, with a toss of indignant astonishment: "Calumniated Innocence run?" For it is singular how in some minds, which are mere bottomless "chaotic whirlpools of gilt shreds," there is no deliberate Lying whatever; and nothing is either believed or disbelieved, but only (with some transient suitable Histrionic emotion) spoken and heard.

Had Dame de Lamotte a certain greatness of character, then; at least, a strength of transcendent audacity, amounting to the bastard-heroic? Great, indubitably great, is her Dramaturgic and Histrionic talent; but as for the rest, one must answer, with reluctance, No. Mrs. Facing-both-ways is a "Spark of vehement Life," but the farthest in the world from a brave woman: she did not, in any case, show the bravery of a woman; did, in many cases, show the mere screaming trepidation of one. Her grand quality is rather to be reckoned negative: the "untamableness" as of a fly; the "wax-cloth dress" from which so much ran down like water. Small sparrows, as I learn, have been trained to fire cannon; but would make poor Artillery Officers in a Waterloo. Thou dost not call that Cork a strong swimmer? Which nevertheless shoots, without hurt, the Falls of Niagara; defies the thunderbolt itself to sink it, for more than a moment. Without intellect, imagination, power of attention, or any spiritual faculty, how brave were one, — with fit motive for it, such as hunger! How much might one dare, by the simplest of methods, by not thinking of it, not knowing it! — Besides, is not Cagliostro, foolish blustering Quack, still here? No scapegoat had ever broader back. The Cardinal too, has he not money? Queen's Majesty, even in effigy, shall not be insulted; the Soubises, De Marsans, and high and puissant Cousins, must huddle the matter up: Calumniated Innocence, in the most universal of Earthquakes, will find *some* crevice to whisk through, as she has so often done.

But all this while how fares it with his Eminence, left somnambulating the *Promenade de la Rose;* and at times truculently stamping? Alas, ill, and ever worse. The starving method, singular as it may seem, brings no capitulation; brings only, after a month's waiting, our tutelary Countess, with a gilt Autograph, indeed, and "all wrapt in silk threads, sealed where they cross,"— but which we read with curses.

We must back again to Paris; there pen new Expostulations; which our unwearied Countess will take charge of, but, alas, can get no answer to. However, is not the 30th of July coming? — Behold, on the 19th of that month, the shortest, most careless of Autographs: with some fifteen hundred pounds of real money in it, to pay the — *interest* of the first instalment; the principal, of some thirty thousand, not being at the moment perfectly convenient! Hungry Boehmer makes large eyes at this proposal; will accept the money, but only as part of payment; the man is positive: a Court of Justice, if no other means, shall get him the remainder. What now is to be done?

Farmer-general Monsieur Saint-James, Cagliostro's disciple, and wet with Tokay, will cheerfully advance the sum needed — for her Majesty's sake; thinks, however (with all his Tokay), it were good to *speak* with her Majesty first. — I observe, meanwhile, the distracted hungry Boehmer driven hither and thither, not by his fixed-idea; alas, no, but by the far more frightful *ghost* thereof, — since no payment is forthcoming. He stands, one day, speaking with a Queen's waiting-woman

(Madame Campan herself), in "a thunder-shower, which neither of them notice,"—so thunderstruck are they. What weather-symptoms for his Eminence!

The 30th of July has come, but no money; the 30th is gone, but no money. O Eminence, what a grim farewell of July is this of **1785**! The last July went out with airs from Heaven, and Trianon Roses. *These* August days, are they not worse than dog's days; worthy to be blotted out from all Almanacs? Boehmer and Bassange thou canst still see; but only "return from them swearing." Nay, what new misery is this? Our tutelary Histrionic Countess enters, distraction in her eyes; she has just been at Versailles; the Queen's Majesty, with a levity of caprice which we dare not trust ourselves to characterize, declares plainly that she will deny ever having got the Necklace; ever having had, with his Eminence, any transaction whatsoever!—Mud-explosion without parallel in volcanic annals.—The Palais de Strasbourg appears to be beset with spies; the Lamottes, for the Count too is here, are packing-up for Bar-sur-Aube. The Sieur Boehmer, has he fallen insane? Or into communication with Minister Breteuil?—

And so, distractedly and distractively, to the sound of all Discords in Nature, opens that Fourth, final Scenic Exhibition, composed by Destiny.

CHAPTER XV.

SCENE FOURTH: BY DESTINY.

It is Assumption-day, the 15th of August. Don thy pontificalia, Grand-Almoner; crush down these hideous temporalities out of sight. In any case, smooth thy countenance into some sort of lofty-dissolute serene:
thou hast a thing they call worshipping God to enact, thyself the first actor.

The Grand-Almoner has done it. He is in Versailles *Œil-de-Bœuf* Gallery; where male and female Peerage, and all Noble France in gala various and glorious as the rainbow, waits only the signal to begin worshipping: on the serene of his lofty-dissolute countenance there can nothing be read. By Heaven! he is sent for to the Royal Apartment!

He returns with the old lofty-dissolute look, inscrutably serene: has his turn for favor actually come, then? Those fifteen long years of soul's travail are to be rewarded by a birth? — Monsieur le Baron de Breteuil issues; great in his pride of place, in this the crowning moment of his life. With one radiant glance, Breteuil summons the Officer on Guard; with another, fixes Monseigneur: "*De par le Roi, Monseigneur:* you are arrested! At *your* risk, Officer!" — Curtains as of pitch-

black whirlwind envelop Monseigneur; whirl off with
him, — to outer darkness. Versailles Gallery explodes
aghast; as if Guy Fawkes's Plot had *burst* under it.
"The Queen's Majesty was weeping," whisper some.
There will be no Assumption-service; or such a one as
was never celebrated since Assumption came in fashion.

Europe, then, shall ring with it from side to side! —
But why rides that Heyduc as if all the Devils drove
him? It is Monseigneur's Heyduc: Monseigneur spoke
three words in German to him, at the door of his Versailles Hotel; even handed him a slip of writing, which,
with borrowed Pencil, "in his red square cap," he had
managed to prepare on the way thither. To Paris! To
the Palais-Cardinal! The horse dies on reaching the
stable; the Heyduc swoons on reaching the cabinet:
but his slip of writing fell from his hand; and I (says
the Abbé Georgel) was there. The red Portfolio, containing all the gilt Autographs, is burnt utterly, with
much else, before Breteuil can arrive for apposition of
the seals! — Whereby Europe, in ringing from side to
side, must worry itself with guessing: and at this hour
on this paper, sees the matter in such an interesting
clear-obscure.

Soon Count Cagliostro and his Seraphic Countess go
to join Monseigneur, in State Prison. In few days, follows Dame de Lamotte, from Bar-sur-Aube; Demoiselle
d'Oliva by-and-by, from Brussels; Villette-de-Rétaux,
from his Swiss retirement, in the taverns of Geneva.
The Bastille opens its iron bosom to them all.

CHAPTER LAST.

MISSA EST.

THUS, then, the Diamond Necklace having, on the one hand, vanished through the Horn Gate of Dreams, and so, under the pincers of Nisus Lamotte and Euryalus Villette, lost its sublunary individuality and being; and, on the other hand, all that trafficked in it, sitting now safe under lock and key, that justice may take cognizance of them, — our engagement in regard to the matter is on the point of terminating. That extraordinary "*Procès du Collier*, Necklace Trial," spinning itself through Nine other ever-memorable Months, to the astonishment of the hundred and eighty-seven assembled *Parlementiers*, and of all Quidnuncs, Journalists, Anecdotists, Satirists, in both Hemispheres, is. in every sense, a "Celebrated Trial," and belongs to Publishers of such. How, by innumerable confrontations and expiscatory questions, through entanglements, doublings and windings that fatigue eye and soul, this most involute of Lies is finally winded off to the scandalous-ridiculous cinder-heart of it, let others relate.

Meanwhile, during these Nine ever-memorable Months, till they terminate late at night precisely with the May of 1786, how many fugitive leaves, quizzical, imaginative, or at least mendacious, were flying about in Newspapers; or stitched together as Pamphlets; and what heaps of others were left creeping in Manuscript, we shall not say; — having, indeed, no complete Collection of them, and what is more to the purpose, little to do with such Collection. Nevertheless, searching for some fit Capital of the composite order, to adorn adequately the now finished singular Pillar of our Narrative, what can suit us better than the following, so far as we know, yet unedited,

Occasional Discourse, by Count Alessandro Cagliostro, Thaumaturgist, Prophet and Arch-Quack; delivered in the Bastille: Year of Lucifer, 5789; of the Mahometan Hegira from Mecca, 1201; of the Cagliostric Hegira from Palermo, 24; of the Vulgar Era, 1785.

"Fellow Scoundrels, — An unspeakable Intrigue, spun from the soul of that Circe-Megæra, by our voluntary or involuntary help, has assembled us all, if not under one roof-tree, yet within one grim iron-bound ring-wall. For an appointed number of months, in the ever-rolling flow of Time, we, being gathered from the four winds, did by Destiny work together in body corporate; and joint laborers in a Transaction already famed over the Globe, obtain unity of Name, like the Argonauts of old, as *Conquerors of the Diamond Necklace.* Erelong it is done (for ring-walls hold not captive the free Scoundrel forever); and we disperse again, over wide terrestrial Space; some of us, it may be, over the very marches of Space. Our Act hangs indissoluble together; floats wondrous in the older and older memory of men : while *we* the little band of Scoundrels, who saw each other, now hover so far asunder, to see each other no more, if not once more only on the universal Doomsday, the Last of the Days !

"In such interesting moments, while we stand within the verge of parting, and have not yet parted, methinks it were well here, in these sequestered Spaces, to institute a few general reflections. Me, as a public speaker, the Spirit of Masonry, of Philosophy, and Philanthropy, and even of Prophecy, blowing mysterious from the Land of Dreams, impels to do it. Give ear, O Fellow Scoundrels, to what the Spirit utters; treasure it in your hearts, practise it in your lives.

"Sitting here, penned-up in this which, with a slight metaphor, I call the Central Cloaca of Nature, where a tyrannical De Launay can forbid the bodily eye free vision, you with the mental eye see but the better. This Central Cloaca, is it not rather a Heart, into which, from all regions, mysterious conduits introduce and forcibly inject whatsoever is choicest in the Scoundrelism of the Earth; there to be absorbed, or again (by the other auricle) ejected into new circulation ? Let the eye of the mind run along this immeasurable venous-arterial system; and astound itself with the magnificent extent of Scoundreldom; the deep, I may say, unfathomable, significance of Scoundrelism.

"Yes, brethren, wide as the sun's range is our Empire, wider than old Rome's in its palmiest era. I have in my time been far; in frozen Muscovy, in hot Calabria, east, west, wheresoever the sky overarches civilized man: and never hitherto saw I myself an alien; out of Scoundreldom I never was. Is it not even said, from of old, by the opposite party: '*All* men are liars'? Do they not (and this nowise 'in haste') whimperingly talk of 'one just person' (as they call him), and of the remaining thousand save one that take part with us? So decided is our majority." — (Applause.)

"Of the Scarlet Woman, — yes, Monseigneur, without offence, — of the Scarlet Woman that sits on Seven Hills, and her Black Jesuit Militia, out foraging from Pole to Pole, I speak not; for the story is too trite: nay, the Militia itself, as I see, begins to be disbanded, and invalided, for a second treachery; treachery to herself! Nor yet of Governments; for a like reason. Ambassadors, said an English punster, *lie* abroad for their masters. Their masters, we answer, lie at home for themselves. Not of all this, nor of Courtship with its Lovers'-vows, nor Courtiership, nor Attorneyism, nor Public Oratory, and Selling by Auction, do I speak: I simply ask the gainsayer, Which is the particular trade, profession, mystery, calling, or pursuit of the Sons of Adam that they successfully manage in the other way? He cannot answer! — No: Philosophy itself, both practical and even speculative, has at length, after shamefullest groping, stumbled on the plain conclusion that Sham is indispensable to Reality, as Lying to Living; that without Lying the whole business of the world, from swaying of senates to selling of tapes, must explode into anarchic discords, and so a speedy conclusion ensue.

"But the grand problem, Fellow Scoundrels, as you well know, is the *marrying* of Truth and Sham; so that they become one flesh, man and wife, and generate these three: Profit, Pudding, and Respectability that always keeps her Gig. Wondrously, indeed, do Truth and Delusion play into one another; Reality rests on Dream. Truth is but the *skin* of the bottomless Untrue: and ever, from time to time, the Untrue *sheds* it; is clear again; and the superannuated True itself becomes a Fable. Thus do all hostile things crumble back into our Empire; and of its increase there is no end.

"O brothers, to think of the Speech without meaning (which is mostly ours), and of the Speech with contrary meaning (which is wholly ours), manufactured by the organs of Mankind in one solar day! Or call it a day of Jubilee, when public Dinners are given, and Dinner-orations are delivered: or say, a Neighboring Island in time of General Election! O ye immortal gods! The mind is lost; can only admire great Nature's plenteousness with a kind of sacred wonder.

"For tell me, What is the chief end of man? 'To glorify God,' said the old Christian Sect, now happily extinct. 'To eat and find. eatables by the readiest method,' answers sound Philosophy, discarding whims. If the method *readier* than this of persuasive-attraction is yet discovered, — point it out! — Brethren, I said the old Christian Sect was happily extinct: as, indeed, in Rome itself, there goes the wonderfullest traditionary Prophecy, of that Nazareth Christ coming back, and being crucified a second time *there;* which truly I see not in the least how he could fail to be. Nevertheless, that old Christian whim, of an actual living and ruling God, and some sacred covenant binding all men in Him, with much other mystic stuff, does, under new or old shape, linger with a few. From these few keep yourselves forever far! They must even be left to their whim, which is not like to prove infectious.

"But neither are we, my Fellow Scoundrels, without our Religion, our Worship; which, like the oldest, and all true Worships, is one of Fear. The Christians have their Cross, the Moslem their Crescent: but have not we too our — Gallows? Yes, *infinitely* terrible is the Gallows; it bestrides with its patibulary fork the Pit of bottomless Terror. No Manicheans are we; our God is One. Great, exceeding great, I say, is the Gallows; of old, even from the beginning, in this world; knowing neither variableness nor decadence; forever, forever, over the wreck of ages, and all civic and ecclesiastic convulsions, meal-mobs, revolutions, the Gallows with front serenely terrible towers aloft. Fellow Scoundrels, fear the Gallows and have no other fear! *This* is the Law and the Prophets. Fear every emanation of the Gallows. And what is every buffet, with the fist, or even with the tongue, of one having authority, but some such emanation? And what is Force of Public Opinion but the infinitude of such emanations, — rushing combined on you, like a mighty storm-wind? Fear the Gallows, I say! O when, with its long black arm, *it* has clutched a man, what avail him all terrestrial things? These pass away, with horrid nameless dinning in his ears; and the ill-starred Scoundrel pendulates between Heaven and Earth, a thing rejected of *both*." — (Profound sensation.)

"Such, so wide in compass, high, gallows-high in dignity, is the Scoundrel Empire; and for depth, it is deeper than the Foundations of the World. For what was Creation itself wholly, according to the best Philosophers, but a Divulsion by the TIME-SPIRIT (or Devil so called); a forceful Interruption, or breaking asunder, of the old Quiescence of Eternity? It was Lucifer that fell, and made this lordly World arise. Deep? It is bottomless-deep; the very Thought, diving, bobs up from it baffled. Is not this that they call Vice of Lying the *Adam-Kadmon*, or primeval Rude-Element, old as Chaos mother's-womb of Death and Hell; whereon their thin film of Virtue, Truth and the like, poorly wavers — for a day? All Virtue, what is it, even by their own showing, but Vice transformed, — that is, manufactured, rendered artificial? 'Man's Vices are the roots from which his Virtues grow out and see the light,' says one: 'Yes,' add I, 'and thanklessly steal their nourishment!' Were it not for the nine hundred ninety and nine unacknowledged, perhaps martyred and calumniated Scoundrels, how were their single Just Person (with a murrain on him!) so much as possible? — Oh, it is high, high: these things are too great for me; Intellect, Imagination, flags her tired wings; the soul lost, baffled" —

— Here Dame de Lamotte tittered audibly, and muttered *Coq-d'Inde*, which, being interpreted into the Scottish tongue, signifies *Bubbly-Jock!* The Arch-Quack, whose eyes were turned inwards as in rapt contemplation, started at the titter and mutter: his eyes flashed outwards with dilated pupil; his nostrils opened wide; his very hair seemed to stir in its long twisted pigtails (his fashion of curl); and as Indignation is said to make Poetry, it here made Prophecy, or what sounded as such. With terrible, working features, and gesticulation not recommended in any Book of Gesture, the Arch-Quack, in voice supernally discordant, like Lions worrying Bulls of Bashan, began:

"Sniff not, Dame de Lamotte; tremble, thou foul Circe-Megæra; thy day of desolation is at hand! Behold ye the Sanhedrim of Judges, with their fanners of written Parchment, loud-rustling, as they winnow all her chaff and down-plumage, and she stands there naked and mean? — Villette, Oliva, do *ye* blab secrets? Ye have no pity of her extreme need; she none of yours. Is thy light-giggling, untamable heart at last heavy? Hark ye! Shrieks of one cast out; whom they brand on both shoulders with iron stamp; the red-hot 'V,' thou *Voleuse*, hath it entered thy soul? Weep, Circe de Lamotte; wail there in truckle-bed, and hysterically gnash thy teeth: nay do, smother thyself in thy door-mat coverlid; thou hast found thy mates; thou art in the Salpêtrière! — Weep, daughter of the high and puissant Sans-inexpressibles! Buzz of Parisian Gossipry is about thee; but not to help thee: no, to eat before thy time. What shall a King's Court do with thee, thou unclean thing, **while thou yet** livest? Escape! Flee to utmost coun-

tries, hide there, if thou canst, thy mark of Cain!—
In the Babylon of Fogland! Ha! is that my London?
See I Judas Iscariot Egalité? Print, yea print abundantly the abominations of your two hearts: breath of
rattlesnakes can bedim the steel mirror, but only for a
time.—And there! Ay, there at last! Tumblest thou
from the lofty leads, poverty-stricken, O thriftless
daughter of the high and puissant, escaping bailiffs?
Descendest thou precipitate, in dead night, from window in the third story; hurled forth by Bacchanals, to
whom thy shrill tongue had grown unbearable? Yea,
through the smoke of that new Babylon thou fallest
headlong; one long scream of screams makes night hideous; thou liest there, shattered like addle egg, 'nigh
to the Temple of Flora!' O Lamotte, has thy *Hypocrisia* ended, then? Thy many characters were all acted.
Here at last thou actest not, but art what thou seemest:
a mangled squelch of gore, confusion and abomination;
which men huddle underground, with no burial-stone.
Thou gallows-carrion!"—

—Here the prophet turned up his nose (the broadest
of the eighteenth century), and opened wide his nostrils
with such a greatness of disgust, that all the audience,
even Lamotte herself, sympathetically imitated him.—
"O Dame de Lamotte! Dame de Lamotte! Now, when
the circle of thy existence lies complete; and my eye
glances over these two score and three years that were
lent thee, to do evil as thou couldst; and I behold thee
a bright-eyed little Tatterdemalion, begging and gathering sticks in the Bois de Boulogne; and also at length

a squelched Putrefaction, here on London pavements; with the head-dressings and hungerings, the gaddings and hysterical gigglings that came between, — *what shall I say was the meaning of thee at all?* —

"Villette-de-Rétaux! Have the catchpoles trepanned thee, by sham of battle, in thy Tavern, from the sacred Republican soil? It is thou that wert the hired Forger of Handwritings? Thou wilt confess it? Depart, unwhipt yet accursed. — Ha! The dread Symbol of our Faith? Swings aloft, on the Castle of St. Angelo, a Pendulous Mass, which I think I discern to be the body of Villette! There let him end; the sweet morsel of our Juggernaut.

"Nay, weep not thou, disconsolate Oliva; blear not thy bright blue eyes, daughter of the shady Garden! Thee shall the Sanhedrim not harm: this Cloaca of Nature emits thee; as notablest of unfortunate-females, thou shalt have choice of husbands not without capital; and accept one. Know this; for the vision of it is true.

"But the Anointed Majesty whom ye profaned? Blow, spirit of Egyptian Masonry, blow aside the thick curtains of Space! Lo you, her eyes are red with their first tears of pure bitterness; not with their last. Tirewoman Campan is choosing, from the Print-shops of the Quais, the reputed-best among the hundred likenesses of Circe de Lamotte: a Queen shall consider if the basest of women ever, by any accident, darkened daylight or candle-light for the highest. The Portrait answers: Never!" — (Sensation in the audience.)

"— Ha! What is *this?* Angels, Uriel, Anachiel,

and ye other five; Pentagon of Rejuvenescence; Power that destroyedst Original Sin; Earth, Heaven, and thou Outer Limbo which men name Hell! Does the EMPIRE OF IMPOSTURE waver? Burst there, in starry sheen, updarting, Light-rays from out *its* dark foundations; as it rocks and heaves, not in travail-throes, but in death-throes? Yea, Light-rays, piercing, clear, that salute the Heavens,— lo, they *kindle* it; their starry clearness becomes as red Hell-fire! IMPOSTURE is in flames, Imposture is burnt up: one Red-sea of Fire, wild-billowing enwraps the World; with its fire-tongue licks at the very stars. Thrones are hurled into it, and Dubois Mitres, and Prebendal Stalls that drop fatness, and — ha! what see I?— all the *Gigs* of Creation: all, all! Woe is me! Never since Pharaoh's Chariots, in the Red-sea of water, was there wreck of Wheel-vehicles like this in the sea of Fire. Desolate, as ashes, as gases, shall they wander in the wind.

"Higher, higher yet flames the Fire-Sea; crackling with new dislocated timber; hissing with leather and prunella. The metal Images are molten; the marble Images become mortar-lime; the stone Mountains sulkily explode. RESPECTABILITY, with all her collected Gigs inflamed for funeral pyre, wailing, leaves the Earth: not to return save under new Avatar. Imposture, how it burns, through generations: how it is burnt up — for a time. The World is black ashes; which, ah, when will they grow green? The Images all run into amorphous Corinthian brass; all Dwellings of men destroyed; the very mountains peeled and riven, the valleys black and dead: it is an empty World! Woe to them that shall be born then!—— A King, a Queen (ah me!) were hurled in; did rustle once; flew aloft, crackling, like paper-scroll. Oliva's Husband was hurled in; Iscariot Egalité; thou grim De Launay, with thy grim Bastille; whole kindreds and peoples; five millions of mutually destroying Men. For it is the End of the Dominion of IMPOSTURE (which is Darkness and opaque Firedamp); and the burning-up, with unquenchable fire, of all the Gigs that are in the Earth!"— Here the Prophet paused, fetching a deep sigh; and the Cardinal uttered a kind of faint, tremulous Hem!

"Mourn not, O Monseigneur, spite of thy nephritic colic and many infirmities. For thee mercifully it was not unto death. O Monseigneur (for thou hadst a touch of goodness), who would not weep over thee, if he also laughed? Behold! The not too judicious Historian, that long years hence, amid remotest wildernesses, writes thy Life, and names thee *Mud-volcano;* even he shall reflect that it *was* thy Life this same; thy *only* chance through whole Eternity; which thou (poor gambler) hast expended *so:* and, even over his hard heart, a breath of dewy pity for thee shall blow.— O Monseigneur, thou wert not all ignoble: thy Mud-volcano was but strength dislocated, fire misapplied. Thou wentest ravening through the world; no Life-elixir or Stone of the Wise could *we* two (for want of funds) discover: a foulest Circe undertook to fatten thee; and thou hadst to fill thy belly with the east wind. And burst? By the Masonry of Enoch, No!

Behold, has not thy Jesuit Familiar his Scouts dim-flying over the deep of human things? Cleared art thou of crime, save that of fixed-idea; weepest, a repentant exile, in the Mountains of Auvergne. Neither shall the Red Fire-sea itself consume thee; only consume thy Gig, and, instead of Gig (O rich exchange!), restore thy Self. Safe beyond the Rhine-stream, thou livest peaceful days; savest many from the fire, and anointest their smarting burns. Sleep finally, in thy mother's bosom, in a good old age!"— The Cardinal gave a sort of guttural murmur, or gurgle, which ended in a long sigh.

"O Horrors, as ye shall be called," again burst forth the Quack, "why have ye missed the Sieur de Lamotte; why not of him, too, made gallows-carrion? Will spear, or sword-stick, thrust at him (or supposed to be thrust), through window of hackney-coach, in Piccadilly of the Babylon of Fog, where he jolts disconsolate, not let out the imprisoned animal existence? Is he poisoned, too? Poison will not kill the Sieur Lamotte; nor steel, nor massacres. Let him drag his utterly superfluous life to a second and a third generation; and even admit the not too judicious Historian to see his face before he die.

"But, ha!" cried he, and stood wide-staring, horror-struck, as if some Cribb's fist had knocked the wind out of him: "O horror of horrors! Is it not Myself I see? Roman Inquisition! Long months of cruel baiting! *Life of Giuseppe Balsamo!* Cagliostro's Body still lying in St. Leo Castle, his *Self* fled — *whither?* By-standers wag their heads, and say: 'The Brow of Brass, behold how it has got all unlacquered; these **Pinchbeck** lips can lie no more!' Eheu! Ohoo!"—And he burst into unstanchable blubbering of tears; and sobbing out the moanfullest broken howl, sank down in swoon; to be put to bed by De Launay and others.

Thus spoke (or thus might have spoken), and prophesied, the Arch-Quack Cagliostro: and truly much better than he ever else did: for not a jot or tittle of it (save only that of our promised Interview with Nestor de Lamotte, which looks unlikelier than ever, for we have not heard of him, dead or living, since 1826) — but has turned out to be literally *true*. As indeed in all this History, one jot or tittle of untruth, that we could render true, is perhaps not discoverable; much as the distrustful reader may have disbelieved.

Here, then, our little labor ends. The Necklace was, and is no more: the stones of it again "circulate in Commerce," some of them perhaps in Rundle's at this hour; and may give rise to what other Histories we know not. The Conquerors of it, every one that trafficked in it, have they not all had their due, which was Death?

This little Business, like a little cloud, bodied itself forth in skies clear to the unobservant: but with such hues of deep-tinted villany, dissoluteness and general delirium as, to the observant, betokened it electric; and wise men, a Goethe for example, boded Earthquakes. Has not the Earthquake come?

NOTES.

CHAPTER I.

PAGE 37, LINE 7. **Improved-drops.** New contrivances for making easy the execution of criminals at Newgate prison, the chief criminal prison of London.

P. 37, l. 9. **Life.** Note the use of capital initial letters throughout this work. What is your opinion of such use?

P. 37, l. 10. **Heyday.** Consult the dictionary for the etymology of this word.

P. 38, l. 1. **Pitifullest.** Carlyle rides ruthlessly over the conventionalities of grammar, and is always ready to sacrifice euphony to force. Note other instances of this formation of the superlative.

P. 38, l. 9. **Pattern-Figure.** Carlyle is fond of applying such descriptive metaphors and figurative nicknames to persons, objects, or events, and having found a good one, repeats it again and again. Thus, he speaks of Gigmanity; constantly calls Rohan a Mud-volcano; and names Madame Lamotte Creative Dramaturgist.

P. 38, l. 15. **Gigman.** Carlyle's footnote here is: " I always considered him a respectable man. — What do you mean by respectable? He kept a Gig." — *Thurtell's Trial*.

P. 39, l. 2. **There is the rub.** Compare Hamlet, Act III., scene I., —

" To die, — to sleep: —
To sleep! perchance to dream; ay, there's the rub."

P. 39, l. 16. **Constitutional History, Philosophy of History,** etc. All terms frequently employed at that time and now to describe the method of writing history in which special attention is given not so much to the facts as to the moral and political lessons taught, or the constitutional development shown by the facts. Dionysus of Halicarnassus says, " History is philosophy teaching by examples."

P. 40, l. 6. **Politico-metaphysical abstraction.** The author's and others' speculations as to the political or moral cause, meaning, and effects of an event in history, rather than the actual historical facts. Carlyle scorned guesses, cant, and sham philosophy. His demand was for Facts, Facts; the truth, not speculations upon the truth.

P. 40, l. 26. **Life-writing.** The etymological translation of "biography," which is derived, through the Greek βιογραφία, from βίος (life) and γράφειν (to write).

P. 40, l. 28. **Boswell,** James (1740–1795), the biographer of Samuel Johnson. His biography, the most famous in the English language, is noted for the minutely truthful picture it gives of Dr. Johnson. Boswell did not spare himself for the sake of "respectability," and his position as reverential reporter of all Johnson's sayings and doings sometimes makes him appear "ridiculous." He has, however, written a true, not a sham, life of the great English man of letters.

P. 41, l. 11. **Charlemague.** The Emperor Charlemagne (742–814) and his paladin, Roland, were the constant themes of song, story, and romance during the Middle Ages. This great emperor did not feel himself above the petty details of caring for his estate. He personally superintended the planting of trees and flowers in his gardens, and gave directions as to what meat and vegetables should be kept in store, and how the poultry and stock should be fed. There is a pretty legend that Eginhard, the secretary of Charlemagne, made love to Emma, the emperor's daughter, and used frequently to visit her secretly in the evening. One evening snow fell while Eginhard was with Emma. Fearing that the tracks of Eginhard's feet in the snow, as he returned, would disclose their intimacy, Emma carried her lover back on her shoulders, knowing that a woman's footprints would excite no curiosity. Charlemagne, however, observed the proceedings from a window, and learning the story of their love, blessed them and consented to their marriage.

In 782, in revenge for a revolt of the Saxons and the consequent defeat and slaughter of several of his captains on the banks of the river Weser, Charlemagne caused 4,500 of the Saxons to be beheaded at a place called Werden, on the river Aller. The story of Roland and how he died in the pass of Roncesvalles should be familiar to all.

P. 41, l. 28. **Turpins and Ariostos.** Turpin is the name given to a fictitious archbishop of Rheims in the time of Charlemagne, to whom was ascribed the authorship of certain Latin prose narratives describing Charlemagne's expedition to Spain and the exploits of Roland. The manuscript was really written in the 11th or 12th century. Ludovicus Ariosto (1474–1533), a famous Italian poet, wrote the great romantic epic poem "Orlando Furioso," the hero of which, Orlando, is identical with Roland.

P. 42, l. 14. **Bright-rolling,** etc. Such compounds are very common in the German language, of which Carlyle was an enthusiastic student. The influence of German literature on his thought and style is very apparent.

P. 42, l. 25. **Real-Phantasmagory.** Phantasmagory, the optical effect produced by the magic lantern. The thought here is, that the different forms of being and the changes of man's life appear before the thoughtful observer as the varied images cast by the magic lantern. The page or more beginning "He has witnessed overhead" is a fine example of Carlyle's power of poetical word-painting when he rises to one of his rapt moods.

P. 43, l. 24. **The Flame-image.** What is meant by this term?

P. 43, l. 30. **Jean Paul.** Johann Paul Friederich Richter (1763–1825), German author and humorist, commonly called Jean Paul. His style is like Carlyle's in many ways, and Carlyle is thought to owe much of his peculiar grotesqueness and figurativeness of style to Richter. At any rate, he read and studied Richter, and contributed essays upon his life and writings to the *Edinburgh Review* (1827) and to the *Foreign Review* (1830).

P. 44, l. 8. **Environment.** Newly coined. The coining of new words is a fault of Carlyle's that young writers should avoid. John Sterling said, referring to Carlyle's writings: "A good deal of the language is positively barbarous. 'Environment,' 'vestural,' 'stertorous,' 'visualized,' 'complected,' and others I think to be found in the first thirty pages are words, so far as I know, without any authority; some of them contrary to analogy; and none repaying by their value the disadvantage of novelty." Some of Carlyle's new words, however, have enriched our language. *Environment*, for example, is a very useful word.

P. 45, l. 24. **Geography,** etc. What is the distinction between geography and topography, and why make the distinction "in this case"?

CHAPTER II.

P. 46, l. 6. **He has long since exchanged his guttural,** etc. Notice the use of the historical present. Carlyle habitually uses it in preference to the past tense, as will be observed throughout this work. *Guttural* is characteristic of the German, as *nasal* of the French. Boehmer had been court jeweller to the King of Saxony before coming to Paris.

P. 46, l. 20. **Ruelle.** The space about the bed in the bed-chamber or alcove, where great personages often received guests and held receptions in the morning before arising. Hence, a private place, "an inner circle." It is derived from the French *rue*, and means, literally, a little, or narrow, street.

P. 47, l. 9. **Joaillier-Bijoutier de la Reine.** Queen's jeweller.

P. 47, l. 14. **Among the Seventies of last Century.** Carlyle's footnote: Except that Madame Campan (*Mémoires*, tome ii.) says the Necklace " was intended for Du Barry," one cannot discover, within many years, the date of its manufacture. Du Barry went " into half pay " on the 10th of May, 1774, — the day when her king died.

P. 47, l. 23. **Did worthy Bassange.** Interrogation is often employed by Carlyle. It serves to excite interest in what is to come and gives variety of expression.

P. 48, l. 21. **Deucalion Deluges,** etc. Deucalion was the classical Noah, and in the Greek mythology he and his wife Pyrrha were the only survivors of the great flood. James Hutton (1726-1797), Scotch geologist, was the author of the Plutonian theory in geology; namely, that the successive rocks of the earth's crust were formed by fusion; that is, through the agency of fire — hence, " explosions." Abraham Gottlieb Werner (1750-1817), German geologist, was the author of the Neptunian theory, that primitive and other rocks were formed by precipitation from *water* — hence, " submersions."

P. 49, l. 2. **Charles the Rash.** Commonly called Charles the Bold, duke of Burgundy. In the reign of Louis XI. of France, the restless ambition of Charles led him to seek independence from the French kingdom. One after another his daring plans were defeated, and he was finally slain at Nancy in 1477. After the battle his body was found frozen in a pool by the roadside.

NOTES. 145

P. 50, l. 10. **Defender of the Faith.** Title of the English sovereign. It was first given by the Pope to Henry VIII. for his defence of the church against Luther.

P. 50, l. 15. **A Heroism,** etc. Is the use of the article before these abstract nouns allowable?

P. 50, l. 17. **Some five or six Books.** Is this statement true? Name the five or six greatest books of the world, in your opinion.

P. 50, l. 21. **Keep it unstolen for fourteen years.** The term of copyright in England formerly was fourteen years. Since 1842 the copyright term has been the life of the author and seven years after. In no case, however, is it to be less than forty-two years, even though the author die before the expiration of that term from the date of copyright.

P. 50, l. 26. **Printseller, of the Rue d'Enfer.** Carlyle's footnote gives some of the authorities he consulted in writing the "Diamond Necklace," as follows: —

Frontispiece of the "*Affaire du Collier*, Paris, 1785;" wherefrom Georgel's Editor has copied it. This "*Affaire du Collier*, Paris, 1785," is not properly a Book; but a bound Collection of such Law-Papers (*Mémoires pour*, etc.) as were printed and emitted by the various parties in that famed "Necklace Trial." These Law-Papers, bound into Two Volumes quarto; with Portraits, such as the Printshops yielded them at the time; likewise with patches of *Ms.*, containing Notes, Pasquinade-songs, and the like, of the most unspeakable character occasionally, — constitute this "*Affaire du Collier;*" which the Paris Dealers in Old Books can still procure there. It is one of the largest collections of Falsehoods that exists in print; and, unfortunately, still, after all the narrating and history there has been on the subject, forms our chief means of getting at the truth of that Transaction. The First Volume contains some Twenty-one *Mémoires pour :* not, of course, Historical statements of truth; but Culprits' and Lawyers' statements of what they wished to be believed; each party *lying* according to his ability to lie. To reach the truth, or even any honest guess at the truth, the immensities of rubbish must be sifted, contrasted, rejected: what grain of historical evidence may lie at the bottom is then attainable. Thus, as this Transaction of the Diamond Necklace has been called the "Largest Lie of the Eighteenth Century," so it comes to us borne, not unfitly, on a whole illimitable dim Chaos of Lies!

Nay, the Second Volume, entitled *Suite de l'Affaire du Collier*, is still stranger. It relates to the Intrigue and Trial of one Bette d'Etienville, who represents himself as a poor lad that had been kidnapped, blindfolded, introduced to beautiful Ladies, and engaged to get husbands for them; as setting out on this task, and gradually getting quite bewitched and bewildered; — most indubitably, going on to bewitch and bewilder other people on all hands of him: the whole *in consequence* of this "Necklace Trial," and the noise it was making! Very curious. The Lawyers did verily busy themselves with this affair of Bette's; there are scarecrow Portraits given, that stood in the Printshops, and no man can know whether the Originals ever so much as existed. It is like the Dream *of* a Dream. The human mind stands stupent; ejaculates the wish that such Gulf of Falsehood would close itself, — before general Delirium supervene, and the Speech of Man become mere incredible, meaningless jargon, like that of choughs and daws. Even from Bette, however, by assiduous sifting, one gathers a particle of truth here and there.

P. 51, l. 19. **Espiegleries.** French — frolicsome tricks.

CHAPTER III.

P. 52, l. 4. **The American War.** The French were then assisting the American Revolution.

P. 52, l. 12. **Savoir-faire.** Skill, tact; literally, knowing how to do.

P. 52, l. 17. **Circulating in commerce.** The expression is quoted from the "Mémoires of Marie Antoinette, by Madame Campan, first lady of the bedchamber to the Queen."

P. 52, l. 17. **Du Barry,** Countess. Notorious and powerful mistress of Louis XV. of France. At the death of Louis XV., in 1774, she retired to St. Cyr, two and one-half miles west of Versailles. She was executed during the Reign of Terror.

P. 53, l. 1. **The Guillotine-axe is forging.** Compare with the opening chapter of Dickens's "Tale of Two Cities." *Tailles* were a kind of feudal tax paid by the subject to the king or overlord, in France; especially, a tax upon the profits of the farmer, estimated by the amount of stock on hand.

P. 53, l. 11. **Pombal,** Marquis de. An eminent Portuguese statesman, minister of foreign affairs 1699-1782. As such he held in check the nobility and removed many abuses.

P. 53, l. 16. **Marie Antoinette.** Queen of France 1774-1792 and wife of Louis XVI. She was born at Vienna, in the imperial castle of Schönbrunn, Nov. 2, 1755, her father being the Emperor Francis I. of Germany, and her mother the famous Maria Theresa. At the age of fourteen she was betrothed to the Dauphin of France. The next year, in April, the prospective bride set out from Vienna and was received at Strasburg with great acclamation by the French people, and with elaborate ceremony by Prince Louis de Rohan, acting as the royal deputy. The marriage ceremony was performed at Versailles, May 16, 1770, Marie Antoinette being not yet fifteen years of age. She became queen in May, 1774, at the accession of her husband to the throne as Louis XVI. She was of a bright, vivacious, simple, and frank nature; was fond of pleasure and fine dress; but despised court etiquette. Not intending to do wrong by her frivolities, she yet had a fatal misconception of the condition of France and of the misery that existed there. Indifferent to the opinions of the court and of the people, she persisted in doing as she pleased; thus offending the court by her contempt of etiquette and disregard for their feelings, and provoking the people by her friendship for unworthy favorites and by making no attempt to court popularity. Her enemies circulated stories about her intrigues, probably all of them false, and she was undoubtedly "more sinned against than sinning." The affair of the Diamond Necklace, in which she was entirely innocent, blasted her good name forever. Her influence over the king in state matters was unfortunate. She took to meddling in public affairs, and opposed most of the measures of reform in the days preceding the Revolution. When the Revolution came, she was the object of passionate hatred on the part of the people. She shared the varying fortunes of her husband during those awful days, and after their imprisonment in the Temple, in 1792, and after the execution of the king, her conduct was most heroic. When the Reign of Terror was at its height, to sate the public appetite for blood, she was dragged before the Revolutionary Tribunal and condemned to death. The next day, Oct. 16, 1793, surrounded by a howling and jeering mob, the once beautiful queen — her hair now turned white by the terrors through which she had passed — was dragged in a tumbrel to the guillotine, and beheaded.

P. 53, l. 22. **Seventy-fours.** Naval vessels carrying seventy-four guns; needed to carry on the war with England.

P. 53, l. 22. **Laudatur et alget.** It is praised and yet is neglected; literally, and yet freezes, grows cold, is not cherished.

P. 53, l. 24. **The Two Sicilies.** Carlyle's note: "See Mémoires de Campan, II., 1–26." Sicily and Naples, under one king until 1870, were called the Two Sicilies.

P. 53, l. 28. **Bankruptcy.** The immediate occasion, and one of the causes, of the French Revolution was the utter bankruptcy of the national treasury. For an account of this see Carlyle's "French Revolution," vol. I., Book II.

P. 54, l. 10. **Irreducible case of Cardan.** Jerome Cardan was a noted mathematician of the sixteenth century. He made many discoveries in algebra and formulated rules for the resolution of cubic equations. An Italian algebraist proposed a question which Cardan could not solve by his rules. Bombelli, an Italian mathematician of the same period, published a work in which he explained the nature of this *irreducible case of Cardan.*

CHAPTER IV.

P. 55, l. 13. **Royal Society** of London. An association of men of learning for the promotion of scientific study and the discussion of scientific subjects. It was founded as early as 1660.

P. 55, l. 14. **Corsican Letitia.** The name of Napoleon Bonaparte's mother, before she married Charles Bonaparte, was Letitia Ramolino.

P. 55, l. 16. **Federations of the Champ de Mars**, etc. The Federation of the Champ de Mars, or Fête of the Federation, was held July 14, 1790, the first anniversary of the fall of the Bastille. It was an elaborate ceremony of peace and good will. All orders took part in it, the king swore to observe and preserve the constitution, and it was the general impression that a new era of peace and reconciliation had been ushered in. See Carlyle's "French Revolution," vol. I. Book I. chapter xii. **September Massacres.** In September, 1792, the news of the advance of the allied forces of Austria and Prussia upon the Revolutionists led to the "Massacres of September." Bands of assassins entered the prisons of Paris, Versailles, Lyons, and other cities, and murdered the prisoners of the Revolution in cold blood. About three thousand were killed. **Bakers' Customers en queue.** Bakers' customers in line, awaiting their turn to buy bread. During the early days of the Revolution the scarcity of bread and the rush for it when the people obtained a little money made it necessary for the crowds at the bakers' shops to form in line, each awaiting his turn to buy. Carlyle describes this in "French Revolution," I., VI., chapter iv. **Danton, Desmoulins,** etc. All leaders in the French Revolution. Robespierre's apparent conscientiousness and reluctance to adopt the death penalty, when contrasted with the horrible scenes of the Reign of Terror, for which he is generally held accountable, have made him, whether justly or not, appear hypocritical. Hence Carlyle likens him to Tartuffe, a celebrated hypocritical pretender to religion, the hero of Molière's comedy of the same name. Marat was at one time a drug clerk.

P. 56, l. 4. **Coadjutor,** etc. A coadjutor was an assistant to a bishop; a Grand Almoner, one of the most powerful officers of the court and the kingdom, by virtue of his office commander of all the orders and director of the great hospital for the blind. A commendator was one who held a living *in commendam;* that is, a vacant living held usually by a bishop until a pastor might be provided, the revenues meanwhile to be collected by the commendator.

P. 56, l. 14. **Siamese Twins.** Eng and Chang, two boys born of Chinese parents in Siam, in 1825, and having their bodies united by a band of flesh stretching from breast bone to breast bone. Both died in 1874, though not at the same time.

P. 56, l. 16. **Rohan,** Louis René Edouard, Cardinal de (1734–1803), the hero and dupe of the Necklace case. The family of Rohan traced its origin to the kings of Brittany and was granted the rank and precedence of a royal princely family by Louis XIV. Members of the family had been archbishops of Strasburg since 1704. Prince Louis was made coadjutor to his uncle, Constantine Rohan-Rochefort, in 1760. He joined the party opposed to the Austrian alliance. In 1772 he went to Vienna as ambassador, and displeased Maria Theresa. He was recalled in 1774. However, through family influence, he was appointed Grand Almoner in 1777, and became Abbot of St. Vaast in 1778, and the same year was made a cardinal. The next year he succeeded his uncle as Archbishop of Strasburg, with an income of 2,500,000 livres. In 1780 he met Cagliostro and lodged him in his palace. After the Necklace trial he was deprived of his office of Grand Almoner and banished to his Abbey of Chaise-Dieu. Allowed to return to Strasburg, in 1789 he was elected to the States General, but in 1791, refusing to take the oath to support the constitution, he went to Germany, where he lived until his death in 1803.

P. 56, l. 24. **Northern Immigrations.** The barbarian invasions of Gaul by the northern German races in the early centuries of the Christian era.

P. 57, l. 5. **Cousin Soubise at Rosbach.** The family of Soubise was related to that of Rohan. Rosbach, or Rossbach, was a small village of Prussian Saxony, where in 1757 Frederick the Great and 22,000 Prussians overwhelmingly defeated the combined French and Imperial army under the Prince of Soubise, an incompetent French general, who held his command only through family influence. Carlyle's footnote reads: "Here is the Epigram they made against him on occasion of Rosbach — in that 'Despotism tempered by Epigrams,' which France was then said to be:

> 'Soubise dit, la lanterne à la main,
> J'ai beau chercher, où diable est mon Armée?
> Elle était là pourtant hier matin :
> Me l'a-t-on prise, ou l'aurais-je égarée? —
>
> Que vois-je, ô ciel! que mon âme est ravie!
> Prodige heureux! la voilà, la voilà! —
> Ah, ventrebleu! qu'est-ce donc que cela?
> Je me trompais, c'est l'Armée Ennemie!'
>   LACRETELLE, ii. 206."

These verses may be translated freely as follows: Soubise, lantern in hand, said, "I have sought in vain — where the devil is my army? Yet it was yonder yesterday morning; has some one stolen it from me, or could I have mislaid it? What do I see, oh heaven, rapture,

rapture! Happy portent! There it is, there it is! Ah, *ventrebleu!* what's that? I made a mistake, it is the enemy's army."

P. 57, l. 23. **Louis the Well-beloved.** The title *Bien-aimé* (well-beloved) was given to Louis XV., when he lay very ill at Metz in 1744. It was bestowed because of the prayerful anxiety of the people for his recovery. The title is the height of irony in view of his subsequent outrageous and infamous reign. See chapter I. of the "French Revolution."

P. 58, l. 6. **Parc-aux-cerfs.** The Deer Park — a name applied in jest to a seraglio established by Louis XV., where some of his debaucheries were carried on.

P. 58, l. 8. **Eu touto nika.** The Greek for "In this conquer." The better known motto is the Latin, "In hoc signo vinces." This was the inscription that Constantine was said to have seen in the heavens, accompanied by the sign of the cross, in consequence of which appearance he embraced Christianity.

P. 58, l. 13. **Macchiavellism.** Political artifice or intrigue employed in upholding despotic government; from the real or supposed principles of government set forth by Macchiavelli, a Florentine statesman of the fifteenth and sixteenth centuries, in his book "The Prince."

P. 58, l. 20. **Back stairs diplomacy.** Private, or officially unrecognized, influence or diplomacy. Royal palaces had two stairways — the public, or state stairway, and a private stairway. Individuals having secret or private business, by having influence with the guardian of the back stairs, could gain access to royalty through that avenue.

P. 58, l. 26. **St. Wast d'Arras.** St. Vaast.

P. 59, l. 8. **M. de Maurepas.** Louis XVI.'s first prime minister.

P. 59, l. 18. **The poor Tit.** The European cuckoo does not build a nest of its own, but lays its eggs in the nests of other birds, to be hatched by the bird in whose nest it is laid. We may imagine the surprise of some small bird, such as the tit, at hatching a stupid cuckoo instead of a child of its own.

P. 59, l. 25. **King Thierri.** *Fainéans* (do-nothings, sluggards) was a name applied to the later Merovingian kings of the Franks who were incompetent, the mayors of the palace being the virtual rulers. Thierry III. was the first, and Childeric III., deposed 730, the last, of the *Fainéans*.

P. 60, l. 26. **Cardinal.** The word is derived from the Latin *cardo* a hinge. "The clerics of the supreme chair are called Cardinals, as undoubtedly adhering more nearly to the hinge by which all things are moved." (Pope Leo IX., quoted in "International Dictionary.")

P. 60, l. 28. **Inhabitant of Saturn.** Fair example of Carlyle's habit of exaggeration.

P. 61, l. 8. **Rouéism.** State, quality, or condition of being a *roué;* that is a person addicted to sensual pleasures, a rake. Carlyle never hesitates to coin a new word, or make a new compound, if it seems useful.

P. 61, l. 18. **Poland a-partitioning.** The first partition of Poland was made in 1772. Catherine the Great of Russia, Frederick the Great of Prussia, and Maria Theresa each seized a portion of the unfortunate country, and after two later partitionings it ceased to exist as a nation.

P. 62, l. 3. **Take her share.** Carlyle's note: *Mémoires de l'Abbé Georgel*, ii. 1–220. Abbé Georgel, who has given, in the place referred to, a long solemn Narrative of the Necklace Business, passes for the grand authority on it: but neither will he, strictly taken up, abide scrutiny. He is vague as may be; writing in what is called the "soaped-pig" fashion: yet sometimes you *do* catch him, and hold him. There are hardly above three dates in his whole Narrative. He mistakes several times; perhaps, once or twice, wilfully misrepresents, a little. The main incident of the business is misdated by him, almost a twelve-month. It is to be remembered that the poor Abbé wrote in exile; and with cause enough for prepossessions and hostilities.

P. 62, l. 5. **Minister D'Aiguillon.** Then prime minister of France.

P. 62, l. 7. **Souper.** Supper.

P. 62, l. 15. **The Scarlet Woman.** Referring to Rome, which is one interpretation of "the woman" in Revelation xvii.

P. 62, l. 28. **Meanwhile Louis the well-beloved.** Louis XV. died of the small-pox, May 10, 1774. Every one had deserted him save a few serving-women. As a signal that he was dead, it is said, a lighted candle was placed in a window of the palace; whereupon the courtiers all rushed, "making a noise absolutely like thunder," to hail the new king, Louis XVI. *Le roi est mort, vive le roi;* the king is dead, long live the king. See the "French Revolution," vol. I., Book I., chapter iv.; also chapter xiii. of the "Diamond Necklace." Louis was buried at St. Denis, the burial-place of the French kings, four and one half miles north of Paris.

P. 63, l. 4. **Amende honorable.** Public apology or reparation for improper language or treatment; a rather mild term to signify repentance before God.

P. 63, l. 17. **Louis XVI.** King of France, 1774–1792, and husband of Marie Antoinette. He was born Aug. 23, 1754, and became king in May, 1774, succeeding his grandfather, Louis XV. He was a man of temperate, moral, and upright character, but was an incompetent king. As dauphin he had, for amusement, learned the trade of locksmith from a mechanic named Gamin, or Gamain, and it would have been well for him had he been born to no higher lot. Louis' intentions were good, but his force of mind and will were weak, and all his good intentions were thwarted by the court and the nobility. The troubled times into which he was born demanded a king of foresight and determination, both of which he lacked. As a result, though the people at first loved him and long wished him no ill, believing him to be misled by his advisers, yet in the stormy days of the Revolution sentiment changed. Louis was deposed September, 1792, and after a farcical trial, in which he bore himself with much fortitude, he met death by the guillotine, Jan. 21, 1793.

P. 63, l. 22. **Heaven and earth.** Carlyle frequently uses exclamations to add force and vivacity to his style.

P. 64, l. 2. **Velocity increasing.** This is the law of falling bodies, for an explanation of which see any text-book on Physics.

P. 64, l. 9. **Comparable to that of Satan.** See Milton's description of Satan's fall in "Paradise Lost," Book I., lines 44–53: —

> "Him the Almighty power
> Hurl'd headlong flaming from th' ethereal sky,
> With hideous ruin and combustion, down
> To bottomless perdition, there to dwell
> In adamantine chains and penal fire,
> Who durst defy the Omnipotent to arms," etc.

P. 64, l. 11. **Choiseul, Wolsey, Racine.** Consult biographical dictionary or encyclopædia.

P. 65, l. 3. **Friar Bacon's head.** Roger Bacon was a famous monk, philosopher, and scientist of the thirteenth century. He is said to have made a brazen head which answered questions. Such heads were made to answer inquiries by the trick of having an assistant concealed, who talked through the long flexible gullet of a crane.

P. 65, l. 10. **Burning marl.**

> His [Satan's] spear . . .
> He walked with to support uneasy steps
> Over the *burning marl.*
> *Paradise Lost*, Book I., lines 292-296.

P. 65, l. 11. **De Marsan, Richelieu,** etc. Noble families that still enjoyed the favor of the court, though he was cast out.

P. 65, l. 24. **Red stockings.** Part of his official dress as cardinal.

P. 65, l. 25. **Garden of Trianon.** The Grand and Petit Trianons were beautiful villas, erected by Louis XIV. and Louis XV., respectively. The Petit (Little) Trianon had a fine garden, with an artificial lake, magnificent trees, a celebrated Hornbeam Arbor, and water-works designed by Lenotre, the famous landscape gardener of the reign of Louis XIV. The Little Trianon had been given to Marie Antoinette by her husband, and was a favorite resort of hers.

P. 65, l. 28. **King's-evil.** Scrofula was so called from the belief that it could be cured by the royal touch. Of course the term is used figuratively here.

P. 65, l. 29. **Campan.** Carlyle's footnote: Madame Campan, in her Narrative, and indeed, in her *Mémoires* generally, does not seem to *intend* falsehood: this, in the Business of the Necklace, is saying a great deal. She rather, perhaps, intends the producing of an impression; which may have appeared to herself to be the right one. But, at all events, she has, here or elsewhere, no notion of historical rigor, she gives hardly any date, or the like; will tell the same thing, in different places, different ways, etc. There is a tradition that Louis XVIII. revised her *Mémoires* before publication. She requires to be read with scepticism everywhere, but yields something in that way.

P. 66, l. 2. **Pillar of salt.** Allusion to Lot's wife ; see Genesis xix.

P. 66, l. 5. **Saverne.** A small town about 300 miles east of Paris and 14 miles from Strasburg; noted for a fine palace, in which Rohan lived at that time.

P. 66, l. 6. **Hope deferred,** etc.   Proverbs xii., 13.

P. 66, l. 12. **To appease the Jews.** Of whom, probably, he had borrowed money without the means of repayment.

P. 66, l. 22. **Cagliostro,** Count Alessandro di, "the arch-quack of the eighteenth century," was born at Palermo, of humble parentage, in 1743. His real name was Giuseppe (Joseph) Balsamo. He seems to have led a wild and abandoned life as a youth. After travelling in Egypt and the East, returning to Italy, he married a pretty young woman of Venice, and the two started out on a career of fraud and knavery. Assuming the title of Count Cagliostro, he travelled through Europe as physician, astrologer, alchemist, magician, philosopher, and exponent of "Egyptian Masonry," the secrets of which he pretended to have discovered in the East. He also did a thriving business in the "elixir of immortal youth." Not only the lower, but the higher classes were duped by him, and in spite of several exposures he continued to prosper. He went to Strasburg in 1780, then to England, and back to Paris in 1785, where he figured in the Necklace case. Thrown into the Bastille, but soon released, he again started out on his knavish travels. But his popularity was on the wane, and upon his visiting Rome, he was tried and condemned to death by the Inquisition for practising Egyptian Masonry. His sentence was commuted to life imprisonment, and he was lodged in the fortress of San Leon, or St. Leo, where he died in 1795.

P. 66, l. 24. **Elective affinity.** A scientific term signifying chemical attraction. Elementary substances by elective affinity are attracted to each other and unite to form chemical compounds.

P. 67, l. 12. **Fripiers.** Literally, second-hand dealers in a small way. The term is applied in an uncomplimentary sense to those who busy themselves in seeking advancement by petty and questionable means.

P. 67, l. 19. **Diderot,** Denis (1713–84), celebrated French philosophical writer, man of letters, and encyclopædist. He was joint editor with D'Alembert of the great French *Encyclopédie,* which had Voltaire and Rousseau as contributors, and exerted a great influence on French thought. Carlyle wrote an essay on Diderot.

P. 68, l. 4. **The Chamois-hunter.** During the close season the killing of chamois was punished by imprisonment in the quicksilver mines. As is well known, the effect of quicksilver, or mercury, upon the system is to cause salivation.

P. 68, l. 8. **With a woful ballad.** From the "seven ages of man," Shakspeare's "As You Like It," Act II., scene vii.,—

> "And then the lover,
> Sighing like furnace, with a woeful ballad
> Made to his mistress' eyebrow."

P. 68, l. 9. **Werter-wise,** like Werther, the hero of Goethe's romance "The Sorrows of Werther." Falling in love with Lotte, his friend's wife, and not being able to conquer his passion, he took his own life.

P. 68, l. 23. **The old nine kingdoms** were England, France, Scotland, Castile, Aragon, Navarre, Sweden, Denmark, Hungary.

CHAPTER V.

P. 70, l. 9. **Nodus.** The knot, intrigue, or plot of a piece.

P. 70, l. 17. **Henri Second.** Henry II. was a dissolute king of France, of the house of Valois. He was accidentally wounded in a tournament, and died from the effects of the wound, in 1559.

P. 70, l. 20. **In vice.** In the place of, as the representative of.

P. 71, l. 19. **Out into the highways to beg.** Carlyle's note: Vie de Jeanne Comtesse de Lamotte (by Herself) vol. I.

P. 71, l. 30. **Suspicious presents.** Carlyle's note: He was of Hebrew descent: grandson of the renowned Jew Bernard, whom Louis XV., and even Louis XIV., used to "walk with in the Royal Garden," when they wanted him to lend them money. See *Souvenirs du Duc de Levis; Mémoires de Duclos,* etc.

P. 72, l. 20. **Leaves of unknown number.** Carlyle's note: Four *Mémoires pour* by her, in this *Affaire du Collier;* like "Lawyers' tongues turned inside out!" Afterwards One Volume, *Mémoires Justificatifs de la Comtesse de,* etc. (London, 1788); with Appendix of "Documents" so-called. This has also been translated into a kind of English. Then Two Volumes, as quoted above: *Vie de Jeanne de,* etc.; printed in London, — by way of extorting money *from Paris.* This latter Lying Autobiography of Lamotte was bought-up by French persons in authority. It was the burning of this *Editio Princeps* in the Sèvres Potteries, on the 30th of May 1792, which raised such a smoke, that the Legislative Assembly took alarm; and had an investigation about it, and considerable examining of Potters, etc., till the truth came out. Copies of the Book were speedily reprinted after the Tenth of August. It is in English too; and, except in the Necklace part, is not so entirely distracted as the former.

P. 73, l. 29. **Gigmanity disgigged.** Both words coined by Carlyle. Gigmanity is a favorite word with him, and means that portion of humanity who slavishly and snobbishly worship this world's goods as the only evidence of respectability and propriety. "Disgigged," of course, means "deprived of its gig;" that is, of its much-worshipped evidences of respectability.

P. 74, l. 1. **Varium et semper mutabile.** See the Latin proverbs, etc., in the appendix of any good dictionary.

P. 74, l. 4. **Rackets and sullens.** A rather "free and easy" use of words, of which, however, Carlyle was entirely capable.

P. 74, l. 9. **Namby-pambying.** Acting in a weakly, sentimental, and affected manner.

P. 74, l. 20. **Uncle Toby.** A noted character and the real hero of Sterne's "Tristram Shandy."

P. 75, l. 9. **We can, etc.** Of course "we" refers to Jeanne. Vividness of description is secured by thus causing the reader to assume the person of Mademoiselle.

P. 75, l. 24. **Minden.** A Prussian town, where, in 1759, Ferdinand, Duke of Brunswick, general of Frederick the Great, defeated the French.

P. 76, l. 16. **Marquis d'Autichamp.** Carlyle's note: He is the same Marquis d'Autichamp who was to "relieve Lyons," and raise the Siege of Lyons, in Autumn 1793, but could not do it.

CHAPTER VI.

P. 78, l. 3. **D'Ormesson, Joly de Fleury, Calonne.** Each was in turn comptroller-general of finances in the reign of Louis XVI., and all failed to manage the finances in a competent manner.

P. 78, l. 8. **Madame of France.** The King's step-sister. Carlyle's note: "See Campan."

P. 78, l. 16. **Drop hints.** Carlyle's note: *Vie de Jeanne de Lamotte, etc. écrite par elle-même,* vol. i.

P. 79, l. 6. **Belle Image.** Madame Campan says: "She lodged at the Belle Image, a very middling, ready-furnished hotel."

P. 79, l. 20. **Elective Franchises.** The right to vote. The extending of the elective franchise in England was a subject of much discussion when Carlyle was writing this work.

P. 80, l. 2. **Atropos.** The third sister of the three Fates. She cut the thread of life when it was completely spun. See "Fates" in dictionary.

P. 80, l. 10. **Tubalcain.** The reputed first worker in metals. See Genesis iv. 22.

P. 80, l. 19. **Valetaille.** Valets; the body of servants, taken collectively.

P. 81, l. 6. **Reformed Parliaments.** England at this time was just passing through a period of agitation for parliamentary reform; that is, the adjustment of the inequalities of parliamentary representation. The Reform Bill passed in 1832. See any English History.

P. 81, l. 26. **Hesperides apples.** That is, golden apples, such as grew in the Garden of the Hesperides. Consult some manual of mythology.

P. 82, l. 2. **Erasmus' ape.** Erasmus, noted Dutch scholar (1467–1536).

P. 82, l. 9. **Burnt cork, etc.** Burnt cork is used in the "make-up" of the face of actors; brayed-resin serves to counterfeit lightning; thunder-barrels produce thunder.

P. 82, l. 15. **Prospero's grotto.** See "The Tempest" of Shakspeare.

P. 82, l. 26. **Drunk Christopher Sly.** The account of the drunken tinker, Christopher Sly, is given in the Induction of Shakspeare's "Taming of the Shrew." He is found dead drunk by a lord and his train, and put into bed. When he awakes, every effort is made to induce him to believe that he has been asleep and dreaming for fifteen years, and that he is not Christopher Sly, but a lord. He finally believes this, and the "Taming of the Shrew" is played for his amusement. "The Sleeper Awakened" is a similar story in the "Arabian Nights."

P. 82, l. 28. **The Gadarenes Swine.** The allusion to the casting out of unclean spirits into swine, as told in Mark v., beginning, "And they came over unto the other side of the sea into the country of the Gadarenes."

P. 83, l. 1. **The Quack of Quacks.** Cagliostro. Hieroglyphic screens, columns, etc., were a part of his mummery. A column was "a lad or young girl who is in the state of innocence; the Venerable communicates to him the power he would have had before the fall of man; which power consists mainly in commanding the pure spirits; the spirits are to the number of seven; it is said they surround the throne; their names are Anael, Michael, Raphael, Gabriel, Uriel, Zobiachel, Anachiel." Quoted by Carlyle in his "Cagliostro."

CHAPTER VII.

P. 84, l. 6. **Queen's Majesty itself.** Carlyle's note: Compare Rohan's *Mémoires pour* (there are four of them), in the *Affaire du Collier*, with Lamotte's four. They go on in the way of controversy, of argument and response.

P. 84, l. 6. **Dost thou bring with thee, etc.** When Hamlet sees his father's ghost he says:

"Be thou a spirit of health, or goblin damned,
Bring with thee airs from heaven, or blasts from hell — "
Hamlet, Act I., Scene iv.

P. 84, l. 12. **As Ephraim did,** etc. "Ephraim feedeth on wind and followeth after the east wind." Hosea xii. 1.

P. 84, l. 21. **Palace Interviews.** Between the Queen and Lamotte. This paragraph is not, of course, a recital of facts, but of what Lamotte represented as facts to Rohan.

P. 85, l. 3. **"Procession of the Blue Ribands."** Carlyle's note: Lamotte's *Mémoires Justificatifs* (London, 1788).

P. 85, l. 10. **On the 21st of March.** The Cardinal's first letter to the Queen (as he supposed) was an apology for his past misconduct and an attempt to excuse it. According to Georgel, "some days afterward she [Lamotte] brought an answer back to him written on a small sheet of gilt-edged paper, in which Marie Antoinette, whose handwriting was successfully imitated, was made to say: 'I have read your letter; I am rejoiced to find you not guilty. At present I am not able to grant you the audience you desire. When circumstances permit you shall be informed of it. Remain discreet.' These few words caused in the cardinal a delirium of satisfaction, which it would be difficult to describe. Madame de Lamotte from that moment was his tutelary angel, who smoothed for him the path of happiness, and from that moment she could have obtained from him anything she desired."

P. 85, l. 16. **Tutelary countess.** Carlyle's note: See *Georgel:* see Lamotte's *Mémoires;* in her Appendix of "Documents" to that volume, certain of these Letters are given.

P. 85, l. 19. **Extraordinary chicken-bowels.** Roman augurs "drew prognostics" from the vital organs of fowls.

P. 85, l. 23. **Malicious Polignacs.** The Duchesse de Polignac was Marie Antoinette's favorite court-lady, attendant, and adviser. Her influence was bad, and she was cordially hated by the populace. Her son, the Prince de Polignac, was at the head of the last ministry of Charles X. When the obnoxious measures of Charles led to the Revolution of July, 1830, and the deposition of Charles, Polignac attempted to escape, but was arrested and imprisoned in the Castle of Ham, an ancient and celebrated fortress in the small French town of that name. Polignac was released in 1836, and died in 1847.

P. 85, l. 29. **At this hour.** Carlyle's note: A.D. 1831.

P. 86, l. 11. **Tenterden Steeple and Godwin Sands.** Tenterden, a market town of Kent, has a church surmounted by a high and massive tower. The name Goodwin (or Godwin) Sands is applied to a dangerous bank of shifting sands, about ten miles long and five to six miles out from the shore of Kent. It is a tradition that these sands were once a low part of the mainland, fenced from the sea by a wall, and that either some stones collected for strengthening the wall, or the funds necessary to keep the wall in repair, were diverted to the building of the tower of Tenterden church. As a result the wall gave way and submerged the land, thus forming Goodwin Sands. Hence the saying arose: "Tenterden steeple was the cause of the Goodwin Sands."

P. 86, l. 18. **Sunt lachrymæ,** etc. There are tears for misfortunes, and human affairs touch the heart. Virgil's Æneid, Book I., line 462.

P. 86, l. 26. **Fouquier Tinville.** The infamous public accuser of the French Revolution.

P. 87, l. 1. **Has mended.** Carlyle's note: Weber: *Mémoires concernant Marie-Antoinette* (London, 1809), tome iii. notes, **106.**

P. 87, l. 13. **Treading the wine-press.** Isaiah lxiii., 3.

P. 87, l. 29. **Saint-Bartholomews, Jacqueries,** etc. All facts or incidents of French history bearing witness to the extravagance, wickedness, or tyranny of the French monarchs. See any history of France or general history. The *gabelle* was a salt-tax. The king had a monopoly of the sale of salt, and every one was compelled to buy seven pounds yearly for each member of the family, whether it was wanted or not. It is said eight thousand persons were imprisoned annually for breaking this law.

CHAPTER VIII.

P. 89, l. 7. **Monsieur le Comte.** That is, M. Lamotte.

P. 89, l. 12. **Desclos.** This valet Desclos, it appears, was the only one connected with the queen's household that Madame Lamotte had ever met. She therefore had her accomplice, Villette, impersonate Desclos in the Necklace matter.

P. 89, l. 22. **Ineffable interview.** Carlyle's note: See *Georgel*.

P. 91, l. 21. **Versailles Treaty.** Sept. 3, 1783, between France, England, and Spain. It recognized the independence of the United States, and surrendered certain English territory to France and to Spain.

P. 92, l. 10. **Cadeau.** A gift, present, complimentary " bonus."

P. 92, l. 17. **Heyduc.** Originally an inhabitant of the Hungarian district of Hadjuc; then a Hungarian soldier; then, as here, a servant in Hungarian uniform.

P. 93, l. 6. **So bounteous,** etc. Carlyle's note: *Georgel*. Rohan's four *Mémoires pour ;* Lamotte's four.

P. 93, l. 11. **The Cloud-Compeller.** Jupiter, who visited Danaë in a shower of gold, and thus became the father of Perseus.

P. 93, l. 30. **Parlement, Grand Chambre and Tournelle.** The Parlement of France was the king's court of justice. It took cognizance of offences against the king, peers, bishops, and higher dignitaries, and there was no appeal from its decisions. These terms all have reference to rooms or judicial organizations connected with secret and unfair inquiry into offences; star-chamber proceedings.

CHAPTER IX.

P. 95, l. 12. **Armida Islands.** Armida is a beautiful enchantress in Tasso's "Jerusalem Delivered." Directed by Satan, she entices Rinaldo to an enchanted island, from which blissful but sensual surroundings he is finally rescued.

P. 95, l. 22. **Descends from her celestial Zodiac.** Allusion to Endymion, a beautiful shepherd youth, whom the goddess Diana visited every night to look upon him as he lay asleep on Mt. Latmos.

P. 97, l. 12. **Peep through the blanket,** etc.

"Come, thick night,
And pall me in the dunnest smoke of hell,
That my keen knife see not the wound it makes,
Nor heaven peep through the blanket of the dark,
To cry, Hold, Hold!"

(*Macbeth*, Act I., scene v.)

P. 97, l. 18. **Linon moucheté.** Dotted lawn.

P. 98, l. 5. **All is safe.** Carlyle's note: Compare *Georgel*, Lamotte's *Mémoires Justificatifs*, and the *Mémoires pour* of the various parties, especially Gay d'Oliva's. Georgel places the scene in the year 1785; quite wrong. Lamotte's "royal Autographs" (as given in the Appendix to *Mémoires Justificatifs*) seem to be misdated as to the day of the month. There is endless confusion of dates.

P. 98, l. 6. **Ixion.** For the story of Ixion see any work on mythology.

P. 98, l. 21. **Highest dalliances.** Carlyle's note: Lamotte's *Mémoires Justificatifs*; Ms. Songs in the *Affaire du Collier*, etc., etc. Nothing can exceed the brutality of these things (unfit for Print or Pen); which nevertheless found believers, — increase of believers, in the public exasperation; and did the Queen, say all her historians, incalculable damage.

P. 98, l. 28. **Philippe Egalité.** Louis Philippe Joseph, Duke of Orleans. Though cousin of Louis XVI. he is believed to have constantly intrigued against him. When the Revolution broke out, he sided with the people against the royalists, and received the title "Egalité" (equality). He voted for the death of Louis XVI., but during the Reign of Terror was himself guillotined in 1793. His son, Louis Philippe, after vicissitudes of fortune, at the "Revolution of

NOTES. 163

1830" was elected "King of the French." His government not being satisfactory, he abdicated in 1848. His death took place in 1850.

P. 99, l. 20. **Beaumarchais.** A noted French dramatist of the time of Louis XVI. His play "Le Mariage de Figaro" had a great popularity and filled the theatre night after night. Carlyle's note here is: Gay d'Oliva's First *Mémoire pour,* p. 37.

CHAPTER X.

P. 100, l. 2. **Partridge the Schoolmaster.** A character in Fielding's novel "Tom Jones." He is shrewd, yet simple and unsophisticated. His simplicity and excitement at the play-house when viewing Garrick's Hamlet are highly entertaining.

P. 100, l. 10. **Nisus and Euryalus.** Firm friends and inseparable companions in Virgil's "Æneid."

P. 100, l. 13. **Through the thicket.** Carlyle's note: See *Lamotte;* see *Gay d'Oliva*.

P. 101, l. 6. **Don Aranda.** An able and powerful Spanish statesman of the eighteenth century. As president of the council of Castile, he expelled the Jesuits from Spain.

P. 101, 14. **Pope Joan.** "John VIII.," said to have been pope 853-855. The probably fictitious account is, that an English girl educated at Cologne assumed man's attire to elope with a monk. Arriving at Rome, she earned a high reputation for learning, and at the death of Leo IV. became pope.

P. 101, l. 15. **Arachne.** She was so skilful at weaving that she challenged Minerva to a trial of skill. Beaten by Minerva, she hanged herself, and the goddess turned her into a spider.

P. 101, l. 22. **Tall, blond and beautiful.** Carlyle's note: I was then presented " to two ladies, one of whom was remarkable for the richness of her shape: she had blue eyes and chestnut hair" (Bette d'Etienville's Second *Mémoire pour;* in the *Suite de l'Affaire du Collier*). This is she whom Bette, and Bette's advocate, intended the world to take for Gay d'Oliva. "The other is of middle size: dark eyes, chestnut hair, white complexion: the sound of her voice is agreeable; she speaks perfectly well, and with no less faculty than vivacity;" this one is meant for Lamotte. Oliva's real name was Essigny; the *Oliva* (OLISVA, anagram of VALOIS) was given her by

Lamotte along with the title of *Baroness* (Ms. Note, *Affaire du Collier*).

P. 101, l. 28. **Palais-Royal.** A famous assemblage of buildings in Paris, consisting of the old palace of the Orleans family, theatres, public gardens, shops, restaurants, etc.

P. 103, l. 18. **Terror.** That is, the Reign of Terror.

CHAPTER XI.

P. 104, l. 8. **Queen's bounty.** The "alms" advanced by Rohan to Madame Lamotte for the queen, which alms the Madame kept.

P. 104, l. 11. **Bend-sinister.** A term of heraldry; a band or stripe crossing the shield diagonally from sinister chief (upper left-hand corner) to dexter base (lower right corner).

P. 104, l. 16. **Worth indeed makes the man.**

> "Worth makes the man, and want of it the fellow,
> The rest is all but leather and prunella."
>
> POPE'S *Essay on Man*.

P. 107, l. 2. **Un beau froid,** etc. Georgel writes: "He arrived most unexpectedly in a fine January frost."

P. 108, l. 28. **For the time being.** Carlyle's note: Campan.

CHAPTER XII.

P. 111, l. 6. **It was said,** etc. Queens sign only with their baptismal names; the signature should have been simply "Marie Antoinette."

P. 111, l. 21. **A glass door.** Carlyle's note: *Georgel*, etc.

P. 112, l. 3. **De par la reine.** In the Queen's name; by the Queen's authority.

P. 112, l. 16. **Horn Gate.** There were two gates through which dreams visited the earth. Through the Horn gate issued true dreams, and through the Ivory gate, false. See Virgil's Æneid, VI., 893.

CHAPTER XIII.

P. 113, l. 5. **"Caraffe and four candles."** More of Cagliostro's mummery. A caraffe is a glass water-bottle.

P. 113, l. 9. **To the glory of Monseigneur.** Carlyle's note: *Georgel*, etc.

P. 114, l. 5. **Œil-de-Bœuf.** "Bull's Eye." A famous ante-chamber of the palace at Versailles and also bedroom of Louis XIV., so called from its oval window. It was the scene of many intrigues.

P. 114, l. 21. **Louvois,** Marquis de (1641–1691), famous war-minister of Louis XIV. At first he had great power over the king, but afterward lost some of his influence. During the laying waste of the Palatinate, when Louis XIV. forbade the burning of Treves, Louvois replied that he had already ordered it burnt to save trouble to the king's conscience. Whereupon Louis, in anger, seized the tongs from the chimney and would have struck his minister had not Madame Maintenon interfered.

P. 114, l. 23. **Maintenon,** Françoise D'Aubigné, Marquise de. One of the most famous personages of the court of Louis XIV. At first governess to Louis' children, she became his friend and companion, and after the death of the queen he privately married her. She had great influence with him and was all-powerful at court. She gave much attention to religion.

P. 114, l. 25. **Maréchaux de France.** Marshals of France. In France a marshal is an officer of the highest military rank.

P. 114, l. 27. **Sound like thunder.** Carlyle's note: *Campan*.

P. 115, l. 12. **She promised it.** Carlyle's note: See *Georgel*.

P. 115, l. 16. **La Reine vient.** The Queen is coming.

P. 116, l. 1. **Mirza's Vision.** The "Vision of Mirza" by Addison is the subject of No. 159 of the *Spectator*. Mirza beholds a wonderful vision of the tide of time, of men crossing the bridge of human life, and of the ocean of eternity, half covered with clouds. When Mirza asked the genius who had called up the vision to let him penetrate the clouds, the vision melted away, and he beheld only "the long hollow valley of Bagdat with oxen, and sheep, and camels grazing upon the side of it."

CHAPTER XIV.

P. 117, l. 5. **Hypocrisia.** The Greek word, ὑποκρόῦα, or ὑπόκρισις, means the playing of a part on the stage; hence our derived meaning of hypocrisy.

P. 117, l. 6. **Mrs. Facing-both-ways.** In the immortal allegory of "Pilgrim's Progress," Bunyan relates the conversation of "Christian" with one "By-ends" from the town of "Fair-speech." When asked the name of his kindred, By-ends replies, "Almost the whole town; and in particular my Lord Turn-about, my Lord Time-server, my Lord Fair-speech, from whose ancestors that town first took its name; also Mr. Smooth-man, *Mr. Facing-both-ways*, Mr. Any-thing; and the parson of our parish, Mr. Two-tongues, was my mother's own brother by father's side."

P. 119, l. 4. **Minister Breteuil.** Minister of the king's household, a personal enemy of Rohan. He and Rohan had been rival applicants for the Vienna embassy, and Rohan had received it.

P. 119, l. 14. **Guy of Warwick.** A famous Anglo-Danish hero, who performed feats of wonderful strength and renown to win the fair Felice.

P. 119, l. 24. **Starve her,** etc. Carlyle's note: See *Lamotte*.

P. 120, l. 5. **In deep treaty,** etc. Carlyle's note: Grey lived in No. 13 New Bond Street; Jeffreys in Piccadilly (Rohan's *Mémoire pour :* see also *Count* de Lamotte's Narrative, in the *Mémoires Justificatifs*). Rohan says, "Jeffreys bought more than 10,000l. worth."

P. 122, l. 8. **We read with curses.** Carlyle's note: See *Lamotte*.

P. 122, l. 22. **Farmer-general Saint James.** A rich financier and disciple of Cagliostro, of whom the Countess and Rohan were hoping to borrow enough money to make the first payment. Saint James was a "new-rich" and was willing to do anything to gain favor at court. A farmer-general (French, *fermier-general*) was one who purchased the right to collect the taxes of a given district. Taxes are still "farmed out" in Turkey.

P. 122, l. 29. **He stands one day,** etc. Carlyle's note: *Campan*.

P. 123, l. 10. **Return from them swearing.** Carlyle's note: *Lamotte*.

P. 123, l. 12. **Distraction in her eyes.** Carlyle's note: *Georgel*.

NOTES. 167

CHAPTER XV.

P. 124, l. 10. **On the serene of his,** etc. Carlyle's note: This is Bette d'Etienville's description of him: "A handsome man, of fifty; with high complexion; hair white-gray, and the front of the head bald: of high stature; carriage noble and easy, though burdened with a certain degree of corpulency; who, I never doubted, was Monsieur de Rohan." (First *Mémoire pour*.)

P. 125, l. 3. **Guy Fawkes's Plot.** See any history of England.

P. 125, l. 11. **Handed him a slip of writing,** etc. Carlyle's note: *Georgel*.

P. 125, l. 29. **The Bastille** was the old state prison in Paris, especially for political prisoners. Its storming by the mob of Paris, July 14, 1789, ushered in the French Revolution. The key of the Bastille was sent to President Washington after the destruction of the prison, and may be seen now at Mt. Vernon. Marquis de Launay was governor of the Bastille at the time of the assault, and was killed after the capture. See Carlyle's "French Revolution."

CHAPTER LAST.

Missa est. From the service of the mass, where the priest says: *Ite,* [*ecclesia*] *missa est* — "The congregation is dismissed." Here, our task is done; finis.

P. 126, l. 21. **Precisely with May 1786.** Carlyle's note: On the 31st of May 1786, sentence was pronounced: about ten at night, the Cardinal got out of the Bastille; large mobs hurrahing round him, — out of spleen to the Court. (See *Georgel*.)

To quote further from the account of the trial: "At length a little after nine in the evening, the decision of the court was made known as follows: —

"1st. The instrument which is the foundation of the suit, with the approvals and annexed signatures, are declared forgeries, and falsely attributed to the queen. 2d. Lamotte, being in contumacy, is condemned to the galleys for life. 3d. Madame de Lamotte to be whipped, branded on the two shoulders with the letter V., and shut up in l'Hopital for life. 4th. Retaux de Villette banished the kingdom for life. 5th. Mademoiselle d'Oliva discharged. 6th. Cagliostro acquitted. 7th. The cardinal acquitted of all suspicion. The injurious accusations against him, contained in the memorial of Madame de Lamotte, suppressed. 8th. The cardinal is allowed to cause the judgment of the court to be printed."

P. 127, l. 17. **Circe-Megæra.** Enchantress-fury. For an account of the enchantress Circe, see Homer's "Odyssey." Megæra was one of the Furies.

P. 129, l. 4. **All men are liars.** Psalm cxvi. 11.

P. 130, l. 28. **Traditionary Prophecy.** Carlyle's note: Goethe mentions it (*Italiänische Reise*).

P. 132, l. 30. **Coq d'Inde.** Turkey-cock; used as a term of mockery, or derision.

P. 133, l. 11. **Bulls of Bashan.** Bashan was a country of Palestine noted for its tall men, its rich pastures, and its large and fat cattle.

P. 133, l. 21. **Voleuse.** Feminine of the French *voleur*, thief. An account of the trial reads: "No sooner did the countess perceive the instruments of her punishment, than she seized one of the executioners by the collar, and bit his hands in such a manner as to take a piece out; fell upon the ground, and suffered more violent convulsions than ever. It was necessary to tear off her clothes to imprint the hot iron upon her shoulders as well as they could."

P. 133, l. 25. **Salpêtrière.** Alms-house and mad-house for women, in Paris. Lamotte escaped after ten days' confinement.

P. 134, l. 6. **Tumblest thou,** etc. Carlyle's note: The English Translator of Lamotte's *Life* says, she fell from the leads of her house, nigh the Temple of Flora, endeavoring to escape seizure for debt, and was taken up so much hurt that she died in consequence. Another report runs that she was flung out of window, as in the Cagliostric text. One way or other she did die, on the 23d of August 1791 (*Biographie Universelle*, xxx. 287). Where the "Temple of Flora" was, or is, one knows not.

P. 134, l. 30. **Bois de Boulogne.** A famous and beautiful park of Paris, covering an area of 2250 acres; a favorite promenade of the Parisians.

P. 135, l. 5. **Villete-de-Retaux.** Carlyle's note: See *Georgel*, and Villette's *Mémoire*.

P. 135, l. 5. **Catchpoles trepanned.** Have the constables ensnared thee?

P. 135, l. 10. **Castle of St. Angelo.** At Rome.

P. 135, l. 14. **Disconsolate Oliva.** Carlyle's note: In the *Affaire du Collier* is this Ms. Note: "Gay d'Oliva, a common-girl of the Palais-Royal, who was chosen to play a part in this Business, got married, some years afterwards, to one Beausire, an Ex-Noble formerly attached to the d'Artois Household. In 1790, he was Captain of the National Guard Company of the Temple. He then retired to Choisy, and managed to be named Procureur of that Commune: he finally employed himself in drawing-up Lists of Proscription in the Luxembourg Prison, when he played the part of informer (*mouton*). See *Tableaux des Prisons de Paris sous Robespierre*." These details are correct. In the *Mémoires sur les Prisons* (new title of the Book just referred to), ii. 171, we find this: "The second Denouncer was Beausire, an Ex-Noble, known under the old government for his intrigues. To give an idea of him, it is enough to say that he married the d'Oliva," etc., as in the Ms. Note already given. Finally is added: "He was the main spy of Boyenval, who, however, said that he made use of him; but that Fouquier-Tinville did not like him, and would have him guillotined in good time."

P. 135, l. 23. **Tirewoman Campan is choosing.** Carlyle's note: see *Campan*.

P. 136, l. 1. **Pentagon of Rejuvenescence.** "In his system he promises his followers to conduct them to perfection, by means of a physical and moral regeneration; . . . by the latter (or moral) to procure them a Pentagon, which shall restore man to his primitive state of innocence, lost by original sin." Quoted in Carlyle's Cagliostro.

P. 136, l. 3. **Empire of Imposture.** The French monarchy with all its false and wicked institutions. The allusion is to the French Revolution.

P. 137, l. 13. **Mourn not, O Monseigneur.** Carlyle's note: Rohan was elected of the Constituent Assembly; and even got a compliment or two in it, as Court-victim, from here and there a man of weak judgment. He was one of the first who, recalcitrating against "Civil Constitution of the Clergy," etc., took himself across the Rhine.

P. 138, l. 13. **Sieur de Lamotte.** Carlyle's note: See Lamotte's Narrative (*Mémoires Justificatifs*).

Lamotte, after his wife's death, had returned to Paris; and been arrested, — *not* for building churches. The Sentence of the old Parliament against him, in regard to the Necklace Business, he gets annulled by the new Courts; but is, nevertheless, "retained in confinement" (*Moniteur* Newspaper, 7th August 1792). He was still in Prison at the time the September Massacre broke out. From Maton de la Varenne we cite the following grim passage: Maton is in La Force Prison.

"At one in the morning" (of Monday, September 3), writes Maton, "the grate that led to our quarter was again opened. Four men in uniform, holding each a naked sabre and blazing torch, mounted to our corridor; a turnkey showing the way; and entered a room close on ours to investigate a box, which they broke open. This done they halted in the gallery; and began interrogating one Cuissa, to know where Lamotte was; who, they said, under pretext of finding a treasure, which they should share in, had swindled one of them out of 300 livres, having asked him to dinner for that purpose. The wretched Cuissa, whom they had in their power, and who lost his life that night, answered, all trembling, that he remembered the fact well, but could not say what had become of the prisoner. Resolute to find this Lamotte and confront him with Cuissa, they ascended into other rooms, and made farther rummaging there; but apparently without effect, for I heard them say to one another: 'Come, search among the corpses then; for, *Nom de Dieu!* we must know what is become of him.'" (*Ma Résurrection, par Maton de la Varenne;* reprinted in the *Histoire Parlementaire,* xviii. 142.) — Lamotte lay in the Bicêtre Prison; but had got out, precisely in the nick of time — and dived beyond soundings.

P. 138, l. 24. **Cribb's fist.** Tom Cribb was a noted English pugilist of the early part of the 19th century.

P. 138, l. 27. **Life of Giuseppe Balsamo.** A "Life of Joseph Balsamo, known as Count Cagliostro," was written in Rome, and purported to contain certain confessions of his.

www.ingramcontent.com/pod-product-compliance
Lightning Source LLC
Chambersburg PA
CBHW022113160426
43197CB00009B/1008